MS-DOS ®
Simplified User Guide

Richard Maran

Hypergraphics Inc.
Mississauga, Ontario, Canada

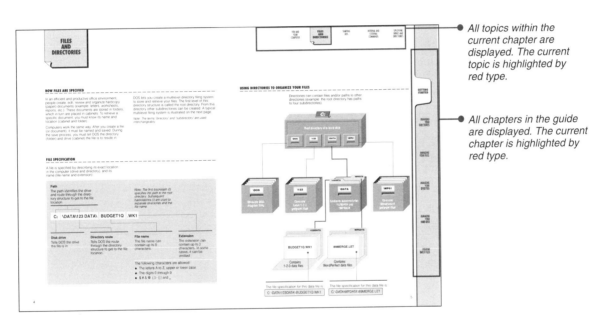

All topics within the current chapter are displayed. The current topic is highlighted by red type.

All chapters in the guide are displayed. The current chapter is highlighted by red type.

HOW TO USE THIS GUIDE

The table of contents is graphically represented on every right facing page. Quickly access the information you require by:

Finding the Chapter

While flipping through the pages of the guide, scan the right hand side of the page to locate the chapter you want.

Finding the Topic within the Chapter

Once you are within the desired chapter, scan the top right hand side of the pages to locate the topic you want. Flip to that high-lighted page.

MS-DOS ®
Simplified User Guide

-- -- -- -- -- -- -- -- -- -- -- --

Copyright©   Hypergraphics Inc. 1990
5755 Coopers Avenue
Mississauga, Ontario
Canada
L4Z 1R9

Published 1990. Second printing 1991.

Canadian Cataloguing in Publication Data

Maran, Richard
   MS-DOS simplified user guide

ISBN 0-9694290-2-9

1. MS-DOS (Computer operating system).
I. Title.

QA76.76.063M37 1990   005.4'46   C90-095082-X

Acknowledgements

-- -- -- -- -- -- -- -- -- -- -- --

Special thanks to Debbie Johnston of the Canadian Imperial Bank of Commerce and to Robert Morris of Deloitte & Touche for their expert guidance on content and technical accuracy.

To the dedicated staff at Hypergraphics Inc. and HyperImage Inc., including Monica DeVries, Eric Feistmantl, Stephen Graetz, Lynne Hoppen, Jim C. Leung, Robert Maran, Ruth Maran, and Elizabeth Seeto for their technical support.

And finally to Maxine Maran for providing the organizational skill to keep the project under control.

Trademark Acknowledgements

dBASE IV is a trademark of Ashton-Tate Corporation.

IBM is a registered trademark and PS/2 is a trademark of International Business Machines Corporation.

Lotus and 1-2-3 are registered trademarks of Lotus Development Corporation.

Microsoft and MS-DOS are registered trademarks of Microsoft Corporation.

WordPerfect is a registered trademark of WordPerfect Corporation.

Cover Design:
Erich Volk

Art Direction:
Elizabeth Seeto

Production:
Jim C. Leung

Linotronic L-300 Output:
HyperImage Inc.

-- -- -- -- -- -- -- -- -- -- -- --

Table of Contents

The Disk Operating System or DOS, is the most important program on your computer. It allows you to control and manage how the computer hardware and software work together.

DOS is a collection of commands that allows the computer to:

● Receive instructions from you

● Work with application programs

● Manage application and data files

● Control and send information to the screen and peripheral devices (example: printers, modems, etc.)

DOS could be described as a computer's central nervous system, or as a traffic manager that keeps everything flowing smoothly.

Whenever your computer is not running some other program, you will be communicating with DOS. You can recognize it by the prompt, C>, that appears on the screen when DOS is ready to accept a command.

Examples

The examples in this guide are based on an IBM or compatible computer with a hard drive (C:) and one floppy drive (A:).

All DOS screen displays are based on DOS Version 4.01.

To install DOS on your hard disk refer to your DOS User's Manual.

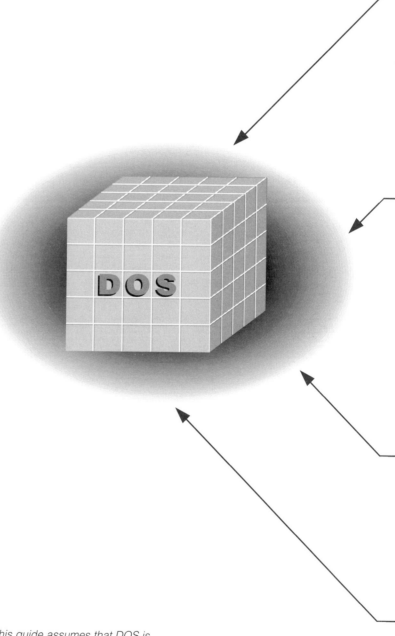

Note: This guide assumes that DOS is already installed on your hard drive, in a subdirectory named \DOS.

| YOU AND YOUR COMPUTER | FILES AND DIRECTORIES | STARTING DOS | INTERNAL AND EXTERNAL COMMANDS | SPECIFYING DRIVES AND DIRECTORIES |

► PERIPHERALS

Other peripherals include modems, plotters, digitizer tablets, mouse, etc.

► SCREEN DISPLAY AND KEYBOARD

You can communicate with DOS and your application programs via the keyboard and monitor.

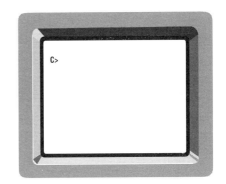

► APPLICATION PROGRAMS

Word Processors	Spreadsheets	Databases
Example: WordPerfect 5.1	Example: Lotus 1-2-3	Example: dBASE IV

► DISK DRIVES

Hard Drives

5.25" Floppy Drives

3.5" Floppy Drives

GETTING STARTED

MANAGING YOUR DIRECTORIES

MANAGING YOUR FILES

MANAGING YOUR DISKETTES

MANAGING YOUR HARD DISK

CREATING BATCH FILES

FILES
AND
DIRECTORIES

HOW FILES ARE SPECIFIED

In an efficient and productive office environment, people create, edit, review and organize hardcopy (paper) documents (example: letters, worksheets, reports, etc.). These documents are stored in folders, which in turn are placed in cabinets. To retrieve a specific document, you must know how to identify it (its name) and its location (cabinet and folder).

Computers work the same way. After you create a file (or document), it must be named and saved. During the save process, you must tell DOS the directory (folder) and drive (cabinet) the file is to reside in.

DOS lets you create a multilevel directory filing system to store and retrieve your files. The first level of this directory structure is called the Root directory. From this directory other subdirectories can be created. A typical multilevel filing system is illustrated on the next page.

Note: The terms "directory" and "subdirectory" are used interchangeably.

FILE SPECIFICATION

A file is specified by describing its exact location in the computer (drive and directory), and its name (file name and extension).

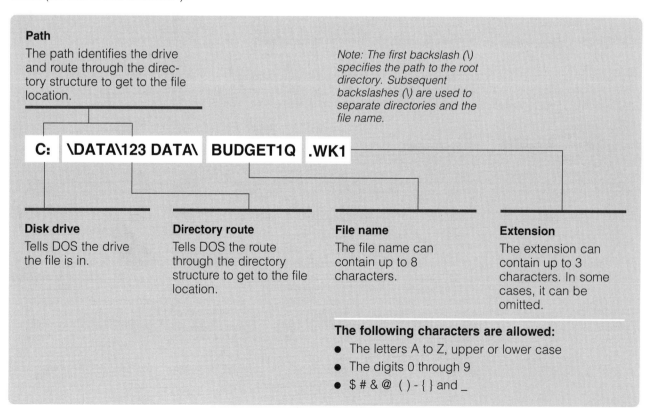

Path

The path identifies the drive and route through the directory structure to get to the file location.

Note: The first backslash (\) specifies the path to the root directory. Subsequent backslashes (\) are used to separate directories and the file name.

C: \DATA\123 DATA\   BUDGET1Q   .WK1

Disk drive

Tells DOS the drive the file is in.

Directory route

Tells DOS the route through the directory structure to get to the file location.

File name

The file name can contain up to 8 characters.

Extension

The extension can contain up to 3 characters. In some cases, it can be omitted.

The following characters are allowed:
- The letters A to Z, upper or lower case
- The digits 0 through 9
- $ # & @ ( ) - { } and _

USING DIRECTORIES TO ORGANIZE YOUR FILES

Directories can contain files and/or paths to other directories (example: the root directory has paths to four subdirectories).

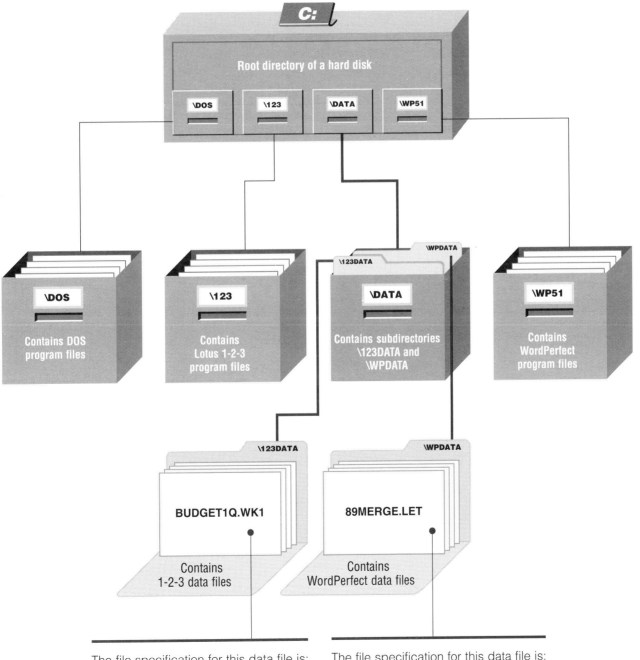

The file specification for this data file is:

C:\DATA\123DATA\BUDGET1Q.WK1

The file specification for this data file is:

C:\DATA\WPDATA\89MERGE.LET

GETTING STARTED

MANAGING YOUR DIRECTORIES

MANAGING YOUR FILES

MANAGING YOUR DISKETTES

MANAGING YOUR HARD DISK

CREATING BATCH FILES

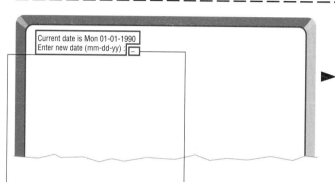

```
Current date is Mon 01-01-1990
Enter new date (mm-dd-yy) : _
```

```
Current date is Mon 01-01-1990
Enter new date (mm-dd-yy) : 3-20-1990_
```

❶ When you turn on the computer it proceeds to do a diagnostic check on itself.

● If the check is OK, the computer beeps and within seconds the above prompt appears.

*Note: If DOS contains a special start-up file called AUTOEXEC.BAT (refer to page 56), a different prompt may appear. For DOS Version 4 or higher, the DOS Shell may appear. If so, press **F3** to return to the system prompt (C>).*

● The blinking line is called a cursor. As you type, text is displayed above the cursor.

Note: Make sure you do not have the DOS diskette in drive A:. If you do, the computer will start DOS from drive A: instead of the hard drive.

❷ If the date is current, press **Enter**.

Note: Most computers contain a battery that keeps the current date and time even when the computer is off.

❸ If the date is incorrect, type the correct date (example: **3-20-1990**) and then press **Enter**.

*Note: If you make a mistake typing the date, press **Backspace** and then retype.*

Restart DOS (called a warm boot)

Hold down **Ctrl** and **Alt** while you press **Del**. The screen clears and DOS is reloaded into the computer. Only take this action when DOS is not responding properly, or when the keyboard locks, preventing data from being entered.

Hard Drive (C:)

This drive is used to store your DOS system files, application programs, data files, utilities, etc.

Floppy Drive (A:)

This drive is used to transfer new progams to your hard disk. It is also used to backup data files created on your hard disk. If your computer has a second floppy drive, it is called (B:).

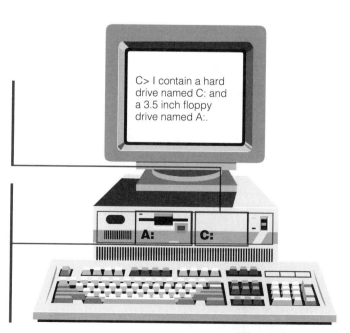

```
C> I contain a hard
drive named C: and
a 3.5 inch floppy
drive named A:.
```

YOU AND
YOUR
COMPUTER

FILES
AND
DIRECTORIES

**STARTING
DOS**

INTERNAL AND
EXTERNAL
COMMANDS

SPECIFYING
DRIVES AND
DIRECTORIES

GETTING
STARTED

MANAGING
YOUR
DIRECTORIES

MANAGING
YOUR FILES

MANAGING
YOUR
DISKETTES

MANAGING
YOUR
HARD DISK

CREATING
BATCH FILES

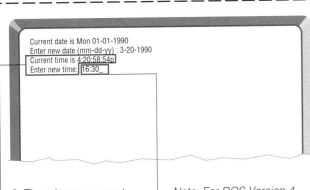

```
Current date is Mon 01-01-1990
Enter new date (mm-dd-yy) : 3-20-1990
Current time is 4:20:58.54p
Enter new time: 16:30_
```

```
Current date is Mon 01-01-1990
Enter new date (mm-dd-yy) : 3-20-1990
Current time is 4:20:58.54p
Enter new time:  16:30

Microsoft (R) MS-DOS(R) Version 4.01
        (C) Copyright Microsoft Corp 1981-1988

C>_
```

● The above prompt
appears.

❹ If the time is correct,
press **Enter**.

or

If the time is incorrect,
type the correct time
(example: **16:30**) and
then press **Enter**.

*Note: For DOS Version 4
or higher you can type
4:30 p.m. as either **16:30**
or **4:30p** (with no spaces
between the 0 and p). If you
leave out the p, DOS
assumes the time is 4:30
a.m.*

● The DOS version,
copyright information
and system prompt (C>)
appear.

● You are now ready to
communicate with DOS.

To clear the screen

Type **CLS** after the C> and then press **Enter**. All
text is cleared off the screen except for the
system prompt C> in the upper left hand corner.

CHECK OR CHANGE THE DATE

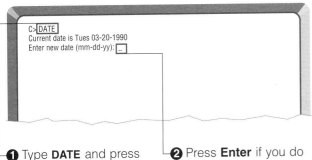

```
C> DATE
Current date is Tues 03-20-1990
Enter new date (mm-dd-yy): □
```

❶ Type **DATE** and press
Enter. The date prompt
appears.

*Note: DOS commands are
not case sensitive. You can
type DATE or date.*

❷ Press **Enter** if you do
not want to change the
date.

or

Type the new date and
then press **Enter**.

CHECK OR CHANGE THE TIME

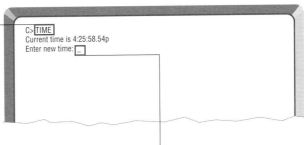

```
C> TIME
Current time is 4:25:58.54p
Enter new time: □
```

❶ Type **TIME** and press
Enter. The time prompt
appears.

❷ Press **Enter** if you do
not want to change the
time.

or

Type the new time and
then press **Enter**.

INTERNAL DOS COMMANDS

EXTERNAL DOS COMMANDS

Internal commands are part of a DOS file called COMMAND.COM. This file is automatically loaded into your computer's internal or active memory when you start DOS. Since all internal commands are resident in active memory, you can issue them from any drive or directory.

External commands are separate files which reside on your hard drive or DOS diskette. They are not kept in active or internal memory, thus the name external. To execute an external command, the computer must read the file from a DOS directory or diskette. However, if the current drive and directory do not contain the DOS files, the computer will not find them.

To issue external commands from any drive or directory, a path command to the DOS files must be included. Refer to the next page for details.

Internal Commands

CD	PROMPT
CLS	REN
COPY	RD
DATE	TIME
ERASE	TYPE
DIR	VER
MD	VOL
PATH	

External Commands

BACKUP	RESTORE
CHKDSK	SORT
DISKCOPY	TREE
FORMAT	XCOPY
MORE	
PRINT	

YOU AND
YOUR
COMPUTER

FILES
AND
DIRECTORIES

STARTING
DOS

**INTERNAL AND
EXTERNAL
COMMANDS**

SPECIFYING
DRIVES AND
DIRECTORIES

SPECIFY A PATH TO EXTERNAL DOS COMMANDS

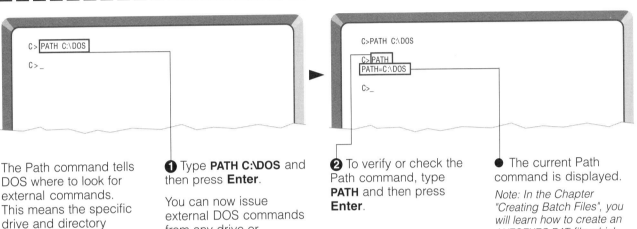

The Path command tells DOS where to look for external commands. This means the specific drive and directory where the DOS files reside.

Note: The Path command can make DOS search more than one directory. To do this you must specify several paths separated by semicolons (example: **PATH C:\DOS;C:\123***).*

❶ Type **PATH C:\DOS** and then press **Enter**.

You can now issue external DOS commands from any drive or directory.

Note: DOS commands are not case sensitive. You can type PATH or path.

To cancel the current path, type **PATH;** *and then press* **Enter***.*

❷ To verify or check the Path command, type **PATH** and then press **Enter**.

● The current Path command is displayed.

Note: In the Chapter "Creating Batch Files", you will learn how to create an AUTOEXEC.BAT file which automatically installs a Path command every time DOS starts the computer.

MANAGING
YOUR
DIRECTORIES

MANAGING
YOUR FILES

MANAGING
YOUR
DISKETTES

Caution

Type DOS commands exactly as shown in the rest of this guide.

Do not add or delete spaces within commands.

C>PATH C:\DOS	Correct
C>PATHC:\DOS	Incorrect
C>PATH C:\DOS;C:\123	Correct
C>PATH C:\DOS; C:\123	Incorrect

DISPLAY THE DOS VERSION NUMBER

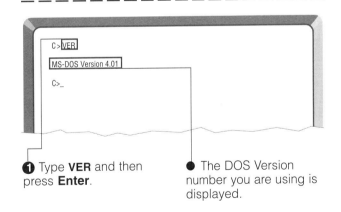

❶ Type **VER** and then press **Enter**.

● The DOS Version number you are using is displayed.

9

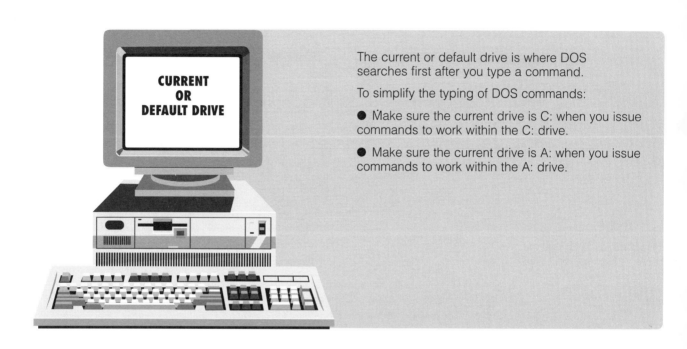

**CURRENT
OR
DEFAULT DRIVE**

The current or default drive is where DOS searches first after you type a command.

To simplify the typing of DOS commands:

● Make sure the current drive is C: when you issue commands to work within the C: drive.

● Make sure the current drive is A: when you issue commands to work within the A: drive.

SPECIFY A DIFFERENT DRIVE

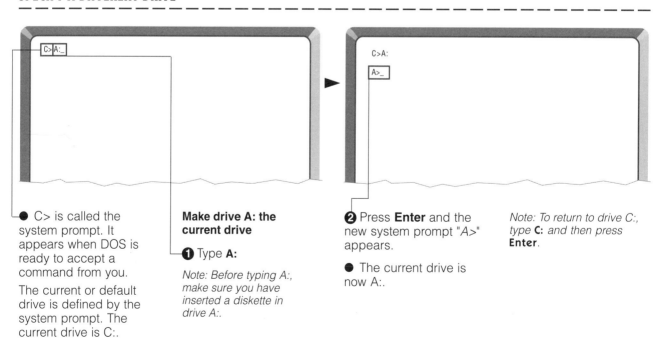

C>A:_

C>A:

A>_

● C> is called the system prompt. It appears when DOS is ready to accept a command from you.

The current or default drive is defined by the system prompt. The current drive is C:.

Make drive A: the current drive

❶ Type **A:**

Note: Before typing A:, make sure you have inserted a diskette in drive A:.

❷ Press **Enter** and the new system prompt "A>" appears.

● The current drive is now A:.

*Note: To return to drive C:, type **C:** and then press **Enter**.*

GETTING STARTED

MANAGING YOUR DIRECTORIES

MANAGING YOUR FILES

MANAGING YOUR DISKETTES

MANAGING YOUR HARD DISK

CREATING BATCH FILES

SPECIFY A DIFFERENT DIRECTORY

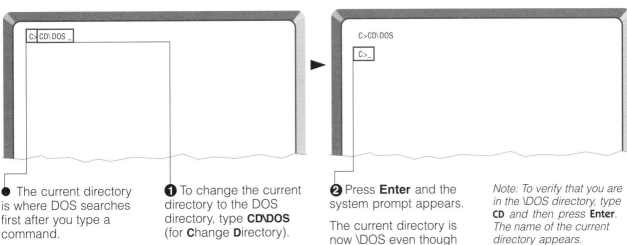

● The current directory is where DOS searches first after you type a command.

❶ To change the current directory to the DOS directory, type **CD\DOS** (for **C**hange **D**irectory).

Note: Refer to page 14 for a full description of the Change Directory command.

❷ Press **Enter** and the system prompt appears.

The current directory is now \DOS even though the system prompt only shows the current drive.

Note: To verify that you are in the \DOS directory, type **CD** *and then press* **Enter**. *The name of the current directory appears.*

CHANGE THE SYSTEM PROMPT TO DISPLAY BOTH THE CURRENT DRIVE AND DIRECTORY

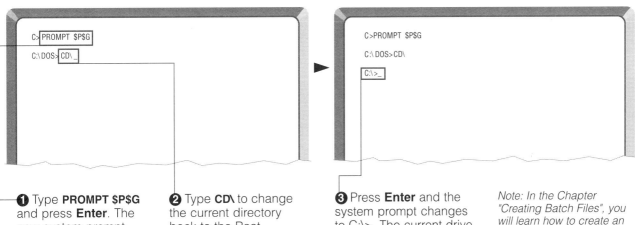

❶ Type **PROMPT PG** and press **Enter**. The new system prompt "C:\DOS>" appears.

Note: The new system prompt "C:\DOS" displays the current drive (C:) and the current directory (\DOS). This is because we changed the current directory to \DOS in the "SPECIFY A DIFFERENT DIRECTORY" example above.

❷ Type **CD** to change the current directory back to the Root directory.

❸ Press **Enter** and the system prompt changes to C:\>. The current drive is still (C:), but the current directory is now the Root directory, defined as (\).

Note: In the Chapter "Creating Batch Files", you will learn how to create an AUTOEXEC.BAT file that automatically specifies the prompt setup as PG every time the computer is turned on.

MAKE
DIRECTORY

DIRECTORY ORGANIZATION

This chart illustrates how a company might organize their PC software and data files on a hard disk.

Note: The terms "directory" and "subdirectory" are used interchangeably.

Subdirectories for DOS, Data and Program files (example: Lotus 1-2-3 and WordPerfect 5.1) are created one level below the Root directory.

Subdirectories for \123DATA and \WPDATA files are created one level below the DATA directory.

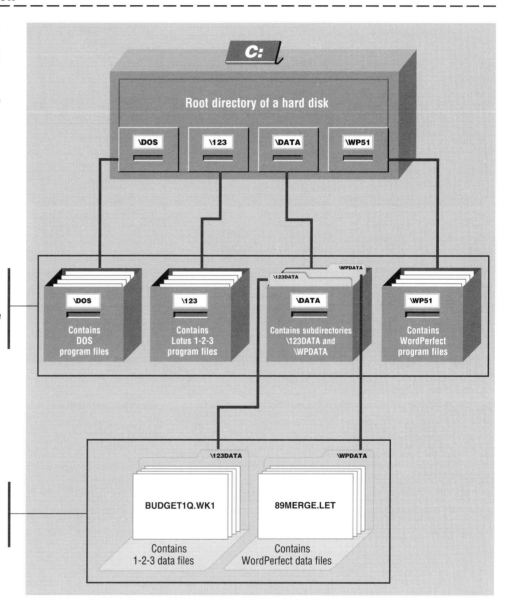

In this directory organization, each program has its own directory. In addition, each program's data files has its own separate directories.

The separation of program files and their respective data files improves your efficiency and productivity when working with large quantities of different kinds of information.

GETTING STARTED

MANAGING YOUR DIRECTORIES

MANAGING YOUR FILES

MANAGING YOUR DISKETTES

MANAGING YOUR HARD DISK

CREATING BATCH FILES

MAKE DIRECTORY

The Make Directory command (typed as MD) allows you to create a multilevel directory filing system.

The screen flow to the right describes how to create the directory structure illustrated on the opposite page.

The Make Directory command is:

MD	PATH	DIRECTORY NAME

PATH	Tells DOS the drive and route through the directory structure to where the new directory is to be created.
DIRECTORY NAME	Tells DOS the name of the new directory to be created.

Note: If you omit the path, new subdirectories are created in the current drive and directory.

```
C:\> MD\DATA
C:\>_
```

Make the DATA directory

❶ Type **MD\DATA** (**MD** stands for **M**ake **D**irectory. **\DATA** is the name of the directory being created).

❷ Press **Enter** and the system prompt "C:\>" appears, indicating that the DATA directory has been created.

*Note: To make the DOS directory, type **MD\DOS**, and press **Enter**. If this directory has already been setup on your machine, the message "Directory already exists" will appear.*

*To make the 123 directory, type **MD\123** and press **Enter**. To make the WP51 directory, type **MD\WP51** and press **Enter**.*

```
C:\>MD\ DATA
C:\> MD\ DATA\123DATA
C:\>_
```

Make the 123DATA directory

❸ Type **MD\DATA\123DATA**

Note: The full path must be typed in order to place \123 DATA inside \DATA.

❹ Press **Enter** and the system prompt "C:\>" appears, indicating that the 123DATA directory has been created.

```
C:\>MD\DATA
C:\>MD\DATA\123DATA
C:\> MD\ DATA\WPDATA
C:\>_
```

Make the WPDATA directory

❺ Type **MD\DATA\WPDATA**

❻ Press **Enter** and the system prompt "C:\>" appears, indicating that the WPDATA directory has been created.

CHANGE
DIRECTORY

CHANGE DIRECTORY

The Change Directory
command (typed as CD)
allows you to change the
current directory to any
other directory.

The current directory on
drive C: can be changed
from any directory to any
other directory using the
Change Directory
command.

*Note: To change from any
directory to the Root
directory, type* **CD** *and
then press* **Enter**.

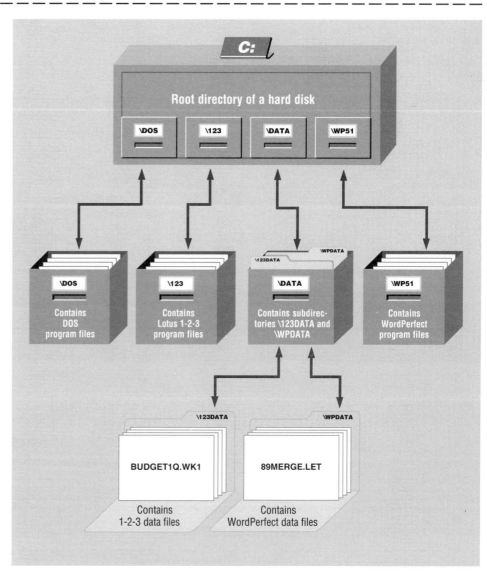

The Change Directory command is:

| CD | PATH |

PATH Tells DOS the drive and route through
the directory structure to the directory
you want to change to.

*Note: If the current drive (example: C:) remains the
same, it can be omitted from the path in the Change
Directory command.*

When you are changing
directories, it is useful for
the system prompt to
display both your current
drive and directory. If
your system prompt is
C>, type **PG**, and then
press **Enter**. The new
system prompt becomes
C:\\>, which displays both
your current drive and
directory. Refer to page
11 for further details.

MAKE
DIRECTORY

**CHANGE
DIRECTORY**

REMOVE
DIRECTORY

TREE

GETTING
STARTED

**MANAGING
YOUR
DIRECTORIES**

MANAGING
YOUR FILES

MANAGING
YOUR
DISKETTES

MANAGING
YOUR
HARD DISK

CREATING
BATCH FILES

CHANGE THE CURRENT DIRECTORY FROM C:\ TO C:\DATA\123DATA

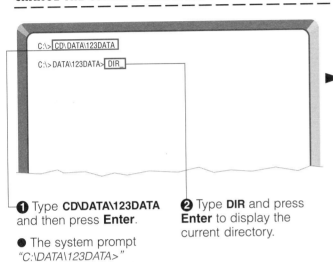

❶ Type **CD\DATA\123DATA** and then press **Enter**.

● The system prompt *"C:\DATA\123DATA>"* appears displaying the new current directory.

❷ Type **DIR** and press **Enter** to display the current directory.

● This line represents the current directory (in this example \DATA\123DATA) and the date and time it was created.

● This line represents the parent of the current directory (in this example \DATA) and the date and time it was created.

MOVE UP ONE DIRECTORY LEVEL (SHORTCUT)

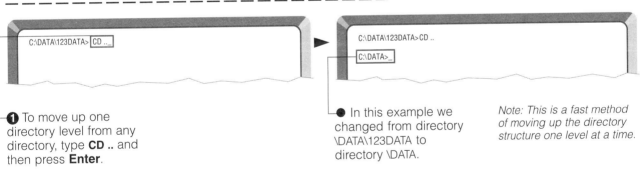

❶ To move up one directory level from any directory, type **CD ..** and then press **Enter**.

● In this example we changed from directory \DATA\123DATA to directory \DATA.

Note: This is a fast method of moving up the directory structure one level at a time.

MOVE DOWN ONE DIRECTORY LEVEL (SHORTCUT)

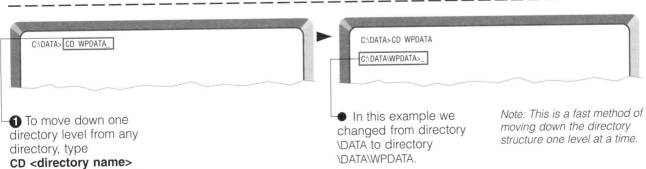

❶ To move down one directory level from any directory, type **CD <directory name>** (example: **CD WPDATA**), and then press **Enter**.

● In this example we changed from directory \DATA to directory \DATA\WPDATA.

Note: This is a fast method of moving down the directory structure one level at a time.

REMOVE
DIRECTORY

REMOVE DIRECTORY

The Remove Directory command (typed as RD) allows you to remove a directory from your multilevel filing structure.

Directories can only be removed starting from the bottom of the file structure and then moving upwards.

This is because a directory can only be removed when it does not contain files or other subdirectories.

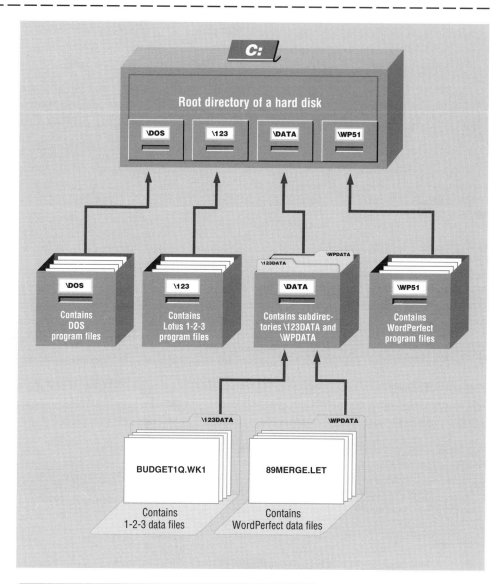

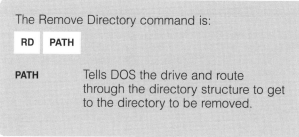

The Remove Directory command is:

| RD | PATH |

PATH   Tells DOS the drive and route through the directory structure to get to the directory to be removed.

MAKE
DIRECTORY

CHANGE
DIRECTORY

REMOVE
DIRECTORY

TREE

REMOVE A DIRECTORY

GETTING
STARTED

MANAGING
YOUR
DIRECTORIES

MANAGING
YOUR FILES

MANAGING
YOUR
DISKETTES

MANAGING
YOUR
HARD DISK

CREATING
BATCH FILES

when the directory does not contain files or subdirectories

```
C:\> RD\DATA\123DATA

C:\>_
```

❶ To remove a directory (example: \123DATA directory), type **RD\DATA\123DATA** and then press **Enter**.

● The system prompt "C:\>" appears indicating that the directory has been removed.

Practice files

Normally, files are created using application software (such as word processing, spreadsheet, graphic packages, etc). The method below should only be used to create practice files.

You can create practice files for this and subsequent pages using the "COPY FROM KEYBOARD" feature described on page 31.

> **Example: Create a file named REVENUE.WK1 and save it to the \DATA\123DATA directory.**
>
> ❶ To change the current directory to \DATA\123DATA, type **CD\DATA\123DATA** and then press **Enter**.
>
> ❷ Type **COPY CON REVENUE.WK1** and then press **Enter**.
>
> ❸ Type a single letter, such as **R**.
>
> ❹ Press **F6** or **Ctrl-Z** (hold down **Ctrl** while you press **Z**). Then press **Enter** and the file is copied to the \DATA\123DATA directory and named REVENUE.WK1.

when the directory contains files or subdirectories

Note: If you need to retain the files in a subdirectory that you intend to remove, copy them to another directory before you delete them.

```
C:\> RD\ DATA\123DATA
Invalid path, not directory,
or directory not empty

C:\>DIR \DATA\123DATA_
```

❶ To remove the \123DATA directory, type **RD\DATA\123DATA** and then press **Enter**.

● A message appears indicating that either files or subdirectories exist within the \123DATA subdirectory.

❷ Type **DIR \DATA\123DATA** and then press **Enter**.

Note: Refer to page 20 for a full description of the Directory command.

```
C:\>RD\ DATA\123DATA
Invalid path, not directory,
or directory not empty

C:\>DIR \DATA\123DATA

Volume in drive C is VOL 01
Volume Serial Number is 2236-1262
Directory of C:\DATA\123DATA

.            <DIR>        03-20-90   10:12a
..           <DIR>        03-20-90   10:12a
REVENUE   WK1     6850    03-20-90    4:20p
INCOME1Q  WK1     2650    03-20-90    1:30p
INCOME2Q  WK1     2850    03-20-90    2:00p
INCOME3Q  WK1     3040    03-20-90    2:40p
       6 File (s)      8898560 bytes free

C:\> ERASE \DATA\123DATA*.*
All files in directory will be deleted!
Are you sure (Y/N)? Y_
```

❸ To erase all data files, type **ERASE \DATA\123DATA*.*** and then press **Enter**.

Note: Refer to page 34 for a full description of the Erase command.

❹ Type **Y** and then press **Enter** to erase the data files.

❺ Repeat from Step **1** above to remove the empty subdirectory.

17

TREE

The Tree command displays the directories and subdirectories in a visually structured format.

Since Tree is an external command, the Path command should include C:\DOS. If it does not, the current drive and directory must be changed to C:\DOS before issuing this command (refer to page 9).

Note: The path C:\DOS can be automatically specified as part of the AUTOEXEC.BAT file (refer to page 56).

The Tree command is:

TREE	DRIVE	PATH	/F

DRIVE   Tells DOS the drive (example: A:, B: or C:) of the directory structure to be displayed.

PATH   Tells DOS the route to the directory for which the tree structure is displayed.

/F   Tells DOS to display all files in the directories.

All examples in this guide are based on the directory structure illustrated below:

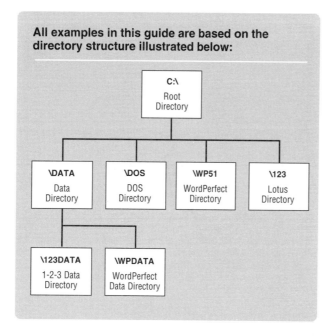

DISPLAY A TREE STRUCTURE STARTING FROM THE ROOT DIRECTORY

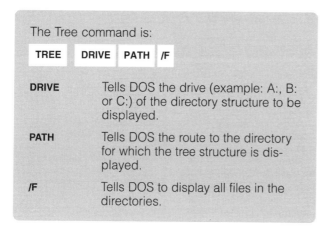

❶ Type **CD\DOS** and then press **Enter** to change the current directory to the \DOS directory.

❷ Type **TREE C:**

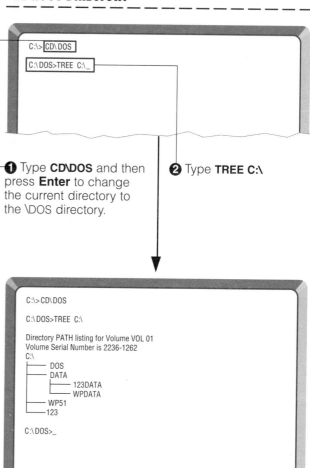

❸ Press **Enter** and the directory tree structure, starting from the Root directory, is displayed.

Note: For DOS Version 3.3 or earlier, the Tree command displays a list of directory names but does not contain the connecting lines.

MAKE
DIRECTORY

CHANGE
DIRECTORY

REMOVE
DIRECTORY

TREE

DISPLAY A TREE STRUCTURE STARTING FROM A SUBDIRECTORY AND INCLUDE ALL FILES ___ ___

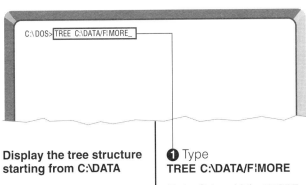

C:\DOS>TREE C:\DATA/F¦MORE_

Display the tree structure starting from C:\DATA

❶ Type
TREE C:\DATA/F¦MORE

Note: Only add the ¦MORE command if you expect the display to exceed one screen.

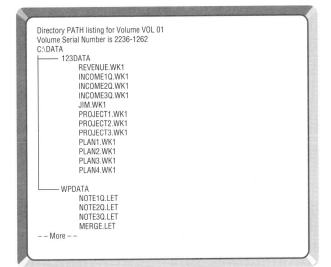

Directory PATH listing for Volume VOL 01
Volume Serial Number is 2236-1262
C:\DATA
└── 123DATA
      REVENUE.WK1
      INCOME1Q.WK1
      INCOME2Q.WK1
      INCOME3Q.WK1
      JIM.WK1
      PROJECT1.WK1
      PROJECT2.WK1
      PROJECT3.WK1
      PLAN1.WK1
      PLAN2.WK1
      PLAN3.WK1
      PLAN4.WK1

└── WPDATA
      NOTE1Q.LET
      NOTE2Q.LET
      NOTE3Q.LET
      MERGE.LET
- - More - -

❷ Press **Enter** and the tree structure, including all directories and files starting from the \DATA directory, is displayed.

❸ Press any key to display the next screen. Continue until all files and directories have been displayed.

PRINT A TREE STRUCTURE STARTING FROM A SUBDIRECTORY AND INCLUDE ALL FILES ___ ___

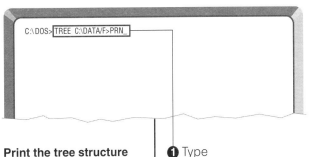

C:\DOS>TREE C:\DATA/F>PRN_

Print the tree structure starting from C:\DATA

❶ Type
TREE C:\DATA/F>PRN and then press **Enter**.

*Note: **>PRN** directs the output to your printer instead of the screen.*

Directory PATH listing for Volume VOL 01
Volume Serial Number is 2236-1262
C:\DATA
└── 123DATA
      REVENUE.WK1
      INCOME1Q.WK1
      INCOME2Q.WK1
      INCOME3Q.WK1
      JIM.WK1
      PROJECT1.WK1
      PROJECT2.WK1
      PROJECT3.WK1
      PLAN1.WK1
      PLAN2.WK1
      PLAN3.WK1
      PLAN4.WK1

└── WPDATA
      NOTE1Q.LET
      NOTE2Q.LET
      NOTE3Q.LET
      MERGE.LET
      PRIMARY.LET
      DO-MON.MEM
      DO-TUE.MEM
      DO-WED.MEM

*Note: Refer to your printer manual to determine if your printer supports the extended character set. If it does not, type **/A** after the Tree command (example: **TREE C:\DATA/F/A>PRN**). This adds vertical bars, hyphens, etc. to help draw the tree structure.*

GETTING
STARTED

MANAGING
YOUR
DIRECTORIES

MANAGING
YOUR FILES

MANAGING
YOUR
DISKETTES

MANAGING
YOUR
HARD DISK

CREATING
BATCH FILES

DIRECTORY

The Directory command (typed as DIR) lists all files in a directory, including information about their size and when they were created or last modified.

You can ask for a listing of all files in a directory, for some of them, or for a single file.

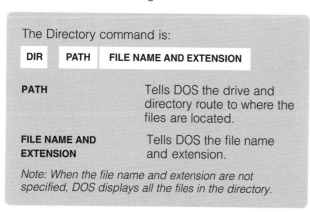

The Directory command is:

DIR	PATH	FILE NAME AND EXTENSION

PATH	Tells DOS the drive and directory route to where the files are located.
FILE NAME AND EXTENSION	Tells DOS the file name and extension.

Note: When the file name and extension are not specified, DOS displays all the files in the directory.

LIST ALL FILES IN A DIRECTORY

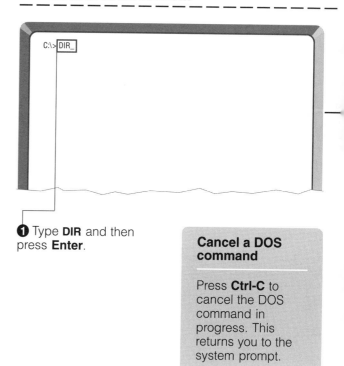

1 Type **DIR** and then press **Enter**.

Cancel a DOS command

Press **Ctrl-C** to cancel the DOS command in progress. This returns you to the system prompt.

LIST ONE FILE IN A DIRECTORY

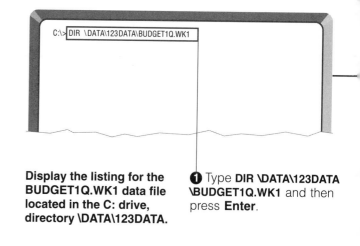

Display the listing for the BUDGET1Q.WK1 data file located in the C: drive, directory \DATA\123DATA.

1 Type **DIR \DATA\123DATA \BUDGET1Q.WK1** and then press **Enter**.

GETTING
STARTED

MANAGING
YOUR
DIRECTORIES

**MANAGING
YOUR FILES**

MANAGING
YOUR
DISKETTES

MANAGING
YOUR
HARD DISK

CREATING
BATCH FILES

```
C:\>DIR

    Volume in drive C is VOL 01
    Volume Serial Number is 2236-1262
    Directory of C:\

COMMAND        COM    37557   04-07-89    12:00a
AUTOEXEC       BAT       84   03-20-90     9:50a
LOTUS          BAT       34   03-20-90     9:55a
WORD51         BAT       42   03-20-90    10:05a
DATA          <DIR>            03-20-90    10:12a
123           <DIR>            03-20-90    10:15a
WP51          <DIR>            03-20-90    10:20a
        7 File(s)         8898560  bytes free
```

● A listing of all files in
the Root directory is
displayed.

● This column lists the
amount of space each
file contains in bytes. A
byte is one character.

● The date and time
files were created or last
modified.

● The total number of
files in the directory and
the amount of space still
available on the disk are
listed.

DOS editing keys

Tab   The cursor moves to the next tab
stop.

Backspace   Moves the cursor back one tab
stop or deletes a single character
to the left of the cursor.

Esc   The current line is cancelled.

The computer remembers the last DOS
command typed. The command can then be
recalled or modified using the F1, F2, or F3
editing keys.

F1   Displays one character at a time
from the last line you entered.

F2   Displays the last line entered up to,
but not including, a specified
character (example: if the last line
entered was DIR AUTOEXEC.BAT
and you pressed **F2**, and then **E**,
the screen would display
DIR AUTO).

F3   Displays the last line entered, or
what remains, if it has been partially
edited.

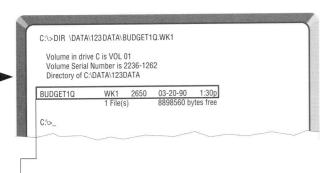

```
C:\>DIR \DATA\123DATA\BUDGET1Q.WK1

    Volume in drive C is VOL 01
    Volume Serial Number is 2236-1262
    Directory of C:\DATA\123DATA

BUDGET1Q       WK1     2650   03-20-90     1:30p
        1 File(s)         8898560  bytes free

C:\>_
```

● DOS displays the
BUDGET1Q.WK1 data file
listing.

21

PAGE DISPLAY MODE /P

When a directory contains more than one screen of files, the Directory command automatically scrolls to the end of the directory.

To view all the files in the directory one screen at a time, the **/P** (for **P**age display) parameter is used.

Note: The examples from this point on in the guide assume that the DOS files are in a directory called \DOS.

Display a directory (example: the DOS directory) one screen at a time.

❶ Type **CD\DOS** and then press **Enter** to change the current directory to the DOS directory.

WIDE DISPLAY MODE /W

To view a directory containing a large number of files across the screen instead of down, the **/W** (for **W**ide display) parameter is used.

Note: The /P and /W options can be used together by typing **DIR/P/W** *or* **DIR/W/P**.

Display a directory (example: the DOS directory) in the wide display mode.

❶ Type **DIR/W** and then press **Enter**.

DIRECTORY · 　　SORT　　　COPY　　　RENAME　　　ERASE　　　TYPE　　　PRINT

GETTING
STARTED

MANAGING
YOUR
DIRECTORIES

MANAGING
YOUR FILES

MANAGING
YOUR
DISKETTES

MANAGING
YOUR
HARD DISK

CREATING
BATCH FILES

```
C:\>CD\DOS

C:\DOS> DIR/P_
```

2 Type **DIR/P** and then press **Enter**.

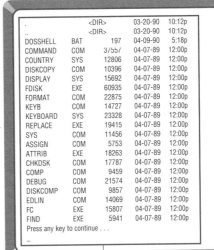

```
.              <DIR>        03-20-90  10:12p
..             <DIR>        03-20-90  10:12p
DOSSHELL  BAT     197       04-09-90   5:18p
COMMAND   COM   37557       04-07-89  12:00p
COUNTRY   SYS   12806       04-07-89  12:00p
DISKCOPY  COM   10396       04-07-89  12:00p
DISPLAY   SYS   15692       04-07-89  12:00p
FDISK     EXE   60935       04-07-89  12:00p
FORMAT    COM   22875       04-07-89  12:00p
KEYB      COM   14727       04-07-89  12:00p
KEYBOARD  SYS   23328       04-07-89  12:00p
REPLACE   EXE   19415       04-07-89  12:00p
SYS       COM   11456       04-07-89  12:00p
ASSIGN    COM    5753       04-07-89  12:00p
ATTRIB    EXE   18263       04-07-89  12:00p
CHKDSK    COM   17787       04-07-89  12:00p
COMP      COM    9459       04-07-89  12:00p
DEBUG     COM   21574       04-07-89  12:00p
DISKCOMP  COM    9857       04-07-89  12:00p
EDLIN     COM   14069       04-07-89  12:00p
FC        EXE   15807       04-07-89  12:00p
FIND      EXE    5941       04-07-89  12:00p
Press any key to continue . . .
_
```

● DOS displays the first screen of files.

3 Press any key to view the second screen of files. Continue until all files have been displayed.

```
C:\DOS> DIR/W

Volume in drive C is VOL 01
Volume Serial No is 2236-1262
Directory of C:\DOS

.                   ..                  DOSSHELL BAT   COMMAND  COM   COUNTRY  SYS
DISKCOPY COM   DISPLAY  SYS   FDISK    EXE   FORMAT   COM   KEYB     COM
KEYBOARD SYS   REPLACE  EXE   SYS      COM   ASSIGN   COM   ATTRIB   EXE
CHKDSK   COM   COMP     COM   DEBUG    COM   DISKCOMP COM   EDLIN    COM
FC       EXE   FILESYS  EXE   FIND     EXE   IFSFUNC  EXE   JOIN     EXE
LABEL    COM   MEM      EXE   MORE     COM   SHARE    EXE   SORT     EXE
SUBST    EXE   TREE     COM   XCOPY    EXE   EMM386   SYS   EXE2BIN  EXE
GWBASIC  EXE   LINK     EXE   PRINT    COM   RAMDRIVE SYS   README   TXT
SMARTDRV SYS   XMA2EMS  SYS   4201     CPI   4208     CPI   5202     CPI
ANSI     SYS   APPEND   EXE   DRIVER   SYS   FASTOPEN EXE   GRAFTABL COM
GRAPHICS COM   GRAPHICS PRO   HIMEM    SYS   MODE     COM   NLSFUNC  EXE
PRINTER  SYS   RECOVER  COM   BACKUP   COM   EGA      CPI   LCD      CPI
RESTORE  COM   EDLIN    EXE   KEYB     COM   SHELL    HLP   SHELL    MEU
SHELL    CLR   SHELLB   COM   SHELLC   EXE
         68 File (s)      8898560 bytes free

C:\DOS>_
```

● DOS displays the directory in wide display format.

Note: To pack more information into the display, the file size and creation date are omitted.

Other ways to halt the display from scrolling

Ctrl-S

Press **Ctrl-S** to temporarily freeze the screen display. Press any key to continue. You can repeat this process until you reach the end of the screen display.

Pause

Press **Pause** to temporarily freeze the screen display. Press any key to continue. You can repeat this process until you reach the end of the screen display.

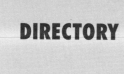

DIRECTORY

USING THE ? WILDCARD

When you use a **?** (question mark) in a file name or extension within a DOS command, the **?** is interpreted to mean any character in that position. This is useful for finding files with similar names.

Note: To create practice files refer to page 17. Make sure you save your files to A:\ (the root directory of the A: drive) for the example on these two pages.

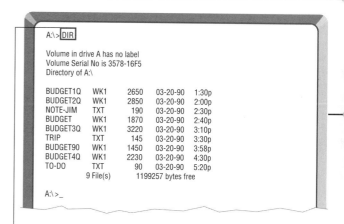

❶ Type **DIR** and then press **Enter** to display all the files in diskette A:.

Note: If the current drive is C, type DIR A:

USING THE * WILDCARD

When you use an ***** (asterisk) in a file name or extension within a DOS command, the ***** is interpreted to mean any number of characters, from one character up to an entire file name or extension. This is useful for finding files containing groups of characters (example: BUDGET, NOTE, TRIP, WK1 etc.).

Note: To display only subdirectories and files without extensions, type DIR *. and then press Enter. This makes it easy to find subdirectories in large directory listings.

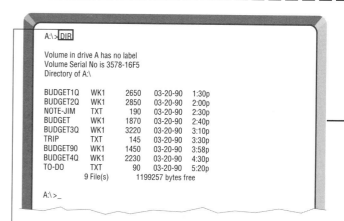

❶ Type **DIR** and then press **Enter** to display all the files in diskette A:

Note: Typing DIR is equivalent to typing DIR *.*

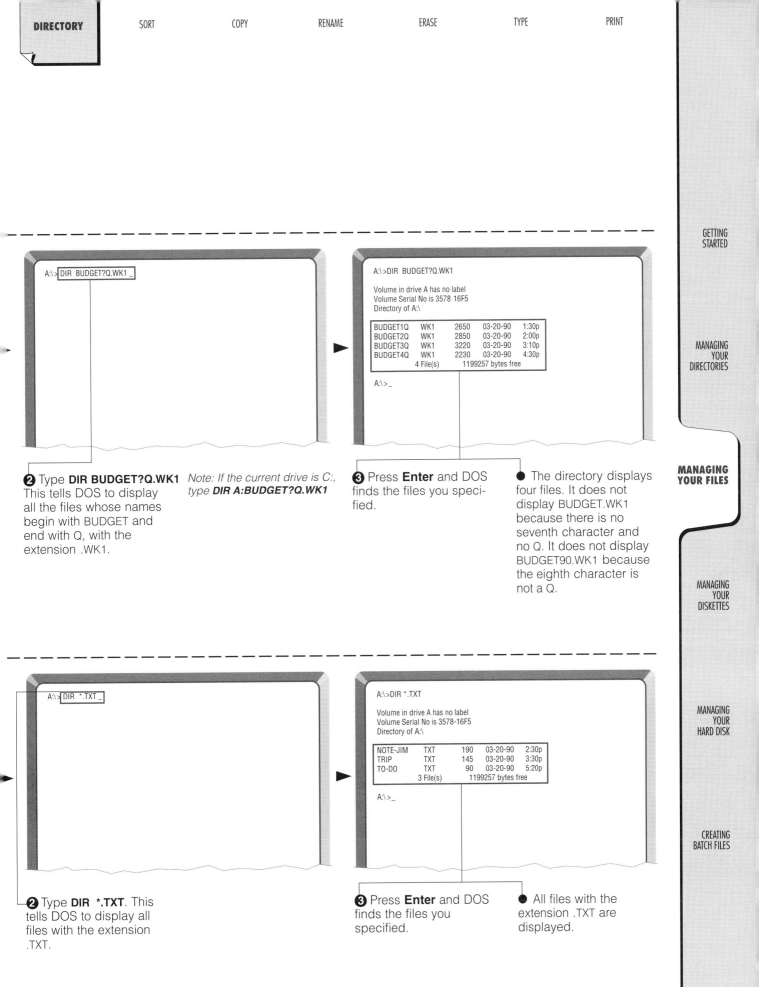

GETTING
STARTED

MANAGING
YOUR
DIRECTORIES

**MANAGING
YOUR FILES**

MANAGING
YOUR
DISKETTES

MANAGING
YOUR
HARD DISK

CREATING
BATCH FILES

A:\>DIR BUDGET?Q.WK1 _

A:\>DIR BUDGET?Q.WK1

Volume in drive A has no label
Volume Serial No is 3578 16F5
Directory of A:\

BUDGET1Q	WK1	2650	03-20-90	1:30p
BUDGET2Q	WK1	2850	03-20-90	2:00p
BUDGET3Q	WK1	3220	03-20-90	3:10p
BUDGET4Q	WK1	2230	03-20-90	4:30p
4 File(s)			1199257 bytes free	

A:\>_

2 Type **DIR BUDGET?Q.WK1**
This tells DOS to display
all the files whose names
begin with BUDGET and
end with Q, with the
extension .WK1.

*Note: If the current drive is C:,
type **DIR A:BUDGET?Q.WK1***

3 Press **Enter** and DOS
finds the files you specified.

● The directory displays
four files. It does not
display BUDGET.WK1
because there is no
seventh character and
no Q. It does not display
BUDGET90.WK1 because
the eighth character is
not a Q.

A:\>DIR *.TXT _

A:\>DIR *.TXT

Volume in drive A has no label
Volume Serial No is 3578-16F5
Directory of A:\

NOTE-JIM	TXT	190	03-20-90	2:30p
TRIP	TXT	145	03-20-90	3:30p
TO-DO	TXT	90	03-20-90	5:20p
3 File(s)			1199257 bytes free	

A:\>_

2 Type **DIR *.TXT**. This
tells DOS to display all
files with the extension
.TXT.

3 Press **Enter** and DOS
finds the files you
specified.

● All files with the
extension .TXT are
displayed.

SORT

The Sort command sorts directory data in alphabetical or numerical order, ascending or descending. The results can be displayed on your screen or be sent directly to your printer.

Since Sort is an external command, the Path command should include C:\DOS. If it does not, the current drive and directory must be changed to C:\DOS before issuing this command (refer to page 9).

Note: The path C:\DOS can be automatically specified as part of the AUTOEXEC.BAT file (refer to page 56).

The Sort command is:

SORT/R/+N

/R Reverses the sort.
       (example: Z to A and 9 to 0)

+N Specifies the column to sort. Values are:

+1	-	for file name
+10	-	for file extension
+16	-	for file size

Note: The +1 can be omitted from the command with the same result (example: SORT/R is the same as SORT/R/+1).

SORT A DIRECTORY BY FILE NAME

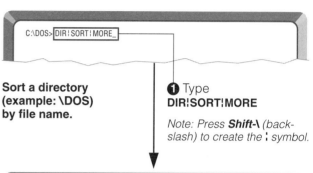

Sort a directory (example: \DOS) by file name.

❶ Type
DIR¦SORT¦MORE

*Note: Press **Shift-** (backslash) to create the ¦ symbol.*

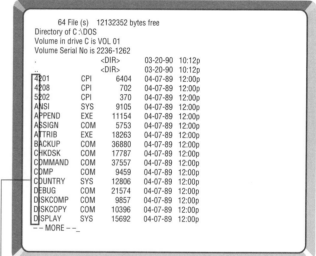

❷ Press **Enter** to display the sorted file names.

Note: Adding ¦MORE to the Sort command displays one screen of files at a time.

❸ Press any key to display more files.

SORT A DIRECTORY BY FILE EXTENSION

C:\DOS> DIR¦SORT/+10¦MORE_

Sort a directory
(example: \DOS)
by file extension.

❶ Type
DIR¦SORT/+10¦MORE

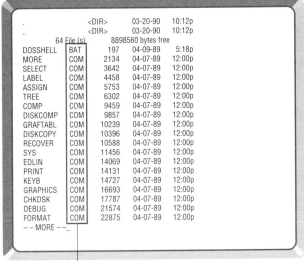

```
                    <DIR>        03-20-90     10:12p
                    <DIR>        03-20-90     10:12p
           64 File (s)        8898560 bytes free
DOSSHELL    BAT       197       04-09-89      5:18p
MORE        COM      2134       04-07-89     12:00p
SELECT      COM      3642       04-07-89     12:00p
LABEL       COM      4458       04-07-89     12:00p
ASSIGN      COM      5753       04-07-89     12:00p
TREE        COM      6302       04-07-89     12:00p
COMP        COM      9459       04-07-89     12:00p
DISKCOMP    COM      9857       04-07-89     12:00p
GRAFTABL    COM     10239       04-07-89     12:00p
DISKCOPY    COM     10396       04-07-89     12:00p
RECOVER     COM     10588       04-07-89     12:00p
SYS         COM     11456       04-07-89     12:00p
EDLIN       COM     14069       04-07-89     12:00p
PRINT       COM     14131       04-07-89     12:00p
KEYB        COM     14727       04-07-89     12:00p
GRAPHICS    COM     16693       04-07-89     12:00p
CHKDSK      COM     17787       04-07-89     12:00p
DEBUG       COM     21574       04-07-89     12:00p
FORMAT      COM     22875       04-07-89     12:00p
-- MORE --_
```

❷ Press **Enter** to display the sorted file extensions.

❸ Press any key to display more files.

SORT A DIRECTORY BY FILE SIZE

C:\DOS> DIR¦SORT/+16¦MORE_

Sort a directory
(example: \DOS)
by file size.

❶ Type
DIR¦SORT/+16¦MORE

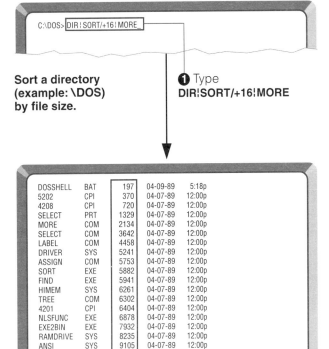

```
DOSSHELL    BAT       197       04-09-89      5:18p
5202        CPI       370       04-07-89     12:00p
4208        CPI       720       04-07-89     12:00p
SELECT      PRT      1329       04-07-89     12:00p
MORE        COM      2134       04-07-89     12:00p
SELECT      COM      3642       04-07-89     12:00p
LABEL       COM      4458       04-07-89     12:00p
DRIVER      SYS      5241       04-07-89     12:00p
ASSIGN      COM      5753       04-07-89     12:00p
SORT        EXE      5882       04-07-89     12:00p
FIND        EXE      5941       04-07-89     12:00p
HIMEM       SYS      6261       04-07-89     12:00p
TREE        COM      6302       04-07-89     12:00p
4201        CPI      6404       04-07-89     12:00p
NLSFUNC     EXE      6878       04-07-89     12:00p
EXE2BIN     EXE      7932       04-07-89     12:00p
RAMDRIVE    SYS      8235       04-07-89     12:00p
ANSI        SYS      9105       04-07-89     12:00p
GRAPHICS    PRO      9397       04-07-89     12:00p
COMP        COM      9459       04-07-89     12:00p
DISKCOMP    COM      9857       04-07-89     12:00p
SMARTDRV    SYS     10224       04-07-89     12:00p
-- MORE --_
```

❷ Press **Enter** to display the sorted file sizes.

❸ Press any key to display more files.

Sort in reverse order and pause every screen

Sort by	Type
File name	DIR¦SORT/R¦MORE
File extension	DIR¦SORT/R/+10¦MORE
File size	DIR¦SORT/R/+16¦MORE

Sort in reverse order and send directly to your printer

Sort by	Type
File name	DIR¦SORT/R>PRN
File extension	DIR¦SORT/R/+10>PRN
File size	DIR¦SORT/R/+16>PRN

GETTING
STARTED

MANAGING
YOUR
DIRECTORIES

**MANAGING
YOUR FILES**

MANAGING
YOUR
DISKETTES

MANAGING
YOUR
HARD DISK

CREATING
BATCH FILES

COPY

The Copy command lets you make duplicates of your files to a different drive/directory or to the same drive/directory.

The Copy command is:

COPY	SOURCE FILE SPECIFICATION	TARGET FILE SPECIFICATION

SOURCE FILE SPECIFICATION   Tells DOS where the file is being copied **from** (path and name).

TARGET FILE SPECIFICATION   Tells DOS where the file is being copied **to** (path and name).

Note: Always change the current drive and directory to where the source file is located.

Applications

● Copying a file to another drive with the same name.

● Copying a file to another drive with a new name.

● Copying several files at once to a new drive.

● Copying a file to the same drive. This is useful if you plan to make changes in the file and want a copy of the original.

Note: The examples that follow are based on the C: drive directory diagram on page 18.

COPY TO A DIFFERENT DRIVE

> **from drive C: to drive A: using the same name**

Suppose you have a file named JIM.WK1 in your C: drive, \DATA\123DATA directory and you want to copy it to the Root directory of diskette A:.

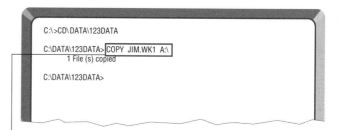

❶ Change the current directory to where the source file is located (example: type **CD\DATA\123DATA** and press **Enter**). The new system prompt *"C:\DATA\123DATA>"* appears.

❷ To copy JIM.WK1 to the Root directory of diskette A:, type:

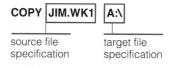

COPY	JIM.WK1	A:\
	source file specification	target file specification

and then press **Enter**.

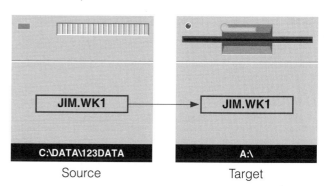

Source   Target

This command copies JIM.WK1 **from** C:\DATA\123DATA (the source), **to** JIM.WK1 on the Root directory of diskette A: (the target).

from drive C: to drive A: using a different name

Suppose you have a file named JIM.WK1 in your C: drive, \DATA\123DATA directory and you want to copy it to the Root directory of diskette A: and name the new copy NOTE1.WK1.

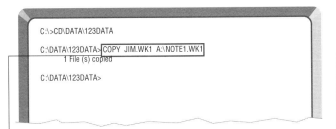

```
C:\>CD\DATA\123DATA

C:\DATA\123DATA> COPY JIM.WK1 A:\NOTE1.WK1
        1 File (s) copied

C:\DATA\123DATA>
```

❶ Change the current directory to where the source file is located (example: type **CD\DATA\123DATA** and press **Enter**). The new system prompt *"C:\DATA\123DATA>"* appears.

❷ To copy JIM.WK1 to the Root directory of diskette A:, with a new file name, type:

COPY ┌JIM.WK1┐ ┌A:\NOTE1.WK1┐

　　　source file　　target file
　　　specification　specification

and then press **Enter**.

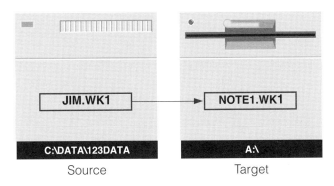

JIM.WK1	→	NOTE1.WK1
C:\DATA\123DATA		**A:**
Source		Target

This command copies JIM.WK1 **from** C:\DATA\123DATA (the source), **to** NOTE1.WK1 on the Root directory of diskette A: (the target).

from drive A: to drive C: using the * wildcard

Suppose you want to copy several worksheets (example: BUDGET1Q.WK1, BUDGET2Q.WK1 and BUDGET3Q.WK1) from the Root directory of diskette A: to your C: drive, \DATA\123DATA directory. If you have used consistent file names, you can use the ***** (asterisk) wildcard.

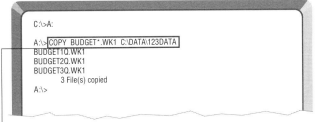

```
C:\>A:

A:\> COPY BUDGET*.WK1 C:\DATA\123DATA
BUDGET1Q.WK1
BUDGET2Q.WK1
BUDGET3Q.WK1
        3 File(s) copied
A:\>
```

❶ Type **A:** and then **Enter** to change the current drive to A. The new system prompt *"A:\>"* appears.

❷ To copy the budget worksheets to the C: drive, \DATA\123DATA directory, type:

COPY ┌BUDGET*.WK1┐ ┌C:\DATA\123DATA┐

　　　source file　　　target file
　　　specification　　specification

and then press **Enter**.

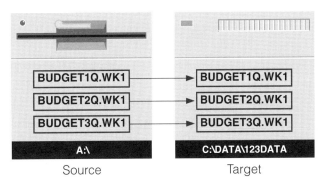

BUDGET1Q.WK1	→	BUDGET1Q.WK1
BUDGET2Q.WK1	→	BUDGET2Q.WK1
BUDGET3Q.WK1	→	BUDGET3Q.WK1
A:		**C:\DATA\123DATA**
Source		Target

This command copies BUDGET1Q.WK1, BUDGET2Q.WK1 and BUDGET3Q.WK1 **from** the Root directory of diskette A:, **to** C:\DATA\123DATA, giving them the same names as the original source files.

GETTING
STARTED

MANAGING
YOUR
DIRECTORIES

**MANAGING
YOUR FILES**

MANAGING
YOUR
DISKETTES

MANAGING
YOUR
HARD DISK

CREATING
BATCH FILES

COPY

COPY TO THE SAME DRIVE

───

| within the same directory | within the same directory using the * (wildcard) |

Suppose you want to copy BUDGET1Q.WK1 within the same directory and name the copy COPY1Q.WK1.

Note: When copying a file within the same directory, a new file name must be specified.

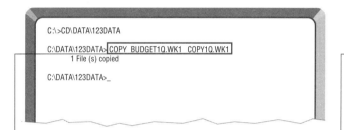

```
C:\>CD\DATA\123DATA

C:\DATA\123DATA> COPY  BUDGET1Q.WK1   COPY1Q.WK1
          1 File (s) copied

C:\DATA\123DATA>_
```

❶ Change the current directory to where the source file is located (example: type **CD\DATA\123DATA** and press **Enter**). The new system prompt *"C:\DATA\123DATA>"* appears.

Note: Since the file is being copied within the same directory, the path can be omitted from the target file specification.

❷ To copy BUDGET1Q.WK1, type:

COPY | BUDGET1Q.WK1 | COPY1Q.WK1

source file specification   target file specification

and then press **Enter**.

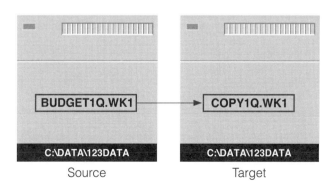

Source   Target

This command copies BUDGET1Q.WK1 **from** C:\DATA\123DATA (the source), **to** COPY1Q.WK1 in the same directory (the target).

Suppose you want to copy several files, (example: NOTE1Q.TXT and NOTE2Q.TXT) to the same directory \DATA\WPDATA, and name them NOTE1Q.NEW and NOTE2Q.NEW.

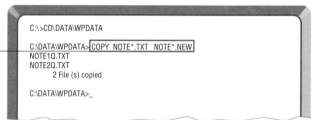

```
C:\>CD\DATA\WPDATA

C:\DATA\WPDATA> COPY  NOTE*.TXT   NOTE*.NEW
NOTE1Q.TXT
NOTE2Q.TXT
          2 File (s) copied

C:\DATA\WPDATA>_
```

❶ Change the current directory to where the source file is located (example: type **CD\DATA\WPDATA** and press **Enter**). The new system prompt *"C:\DATA\WPDATA>"* appears.

Note: Since the file is being copied within the same directory, the path can be omitted from the target file specification.

❷ To copy NOTE*.TXT, type:

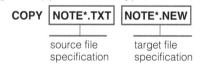

COPY | NOTE*.TXT | NOTE*.NEW

source file specification   target file specification

and then press **Enter**.

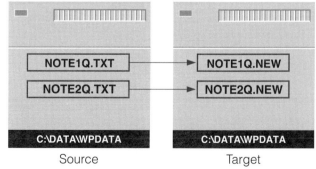

Source   Target

This command copies NOTE1Q.TXT and NOTE2Q.TXT **from** C:\DATA\WPDATA (the source), **to** NOTE1Q.NEW and NOTE2Q.NEW in the same directory (the target).

GETTING
STARTED

MANAGING
YOUR
DIRECTORIES

**MANAGING
YOUR FILES**

MANAGING
YOUR
DISKETTES

MANAGING
YOUR
HARD DISK

CREATING
BATCH FILES

COPY FROM THE KEYBOARD

to another directory

Suppose you want to copy the file COMMAND.COM from the Root directory to the \DOS directory.

❶ To copy COMMAND.COM, type:

source file   target file
specification   specification

and then press **Enter**.

Note: The target drive C: is the same as the current drive so, it can be omitted from the target file specification. Also, since the name of the copied file is to be the same on the target, it can be omitted from the file specification.

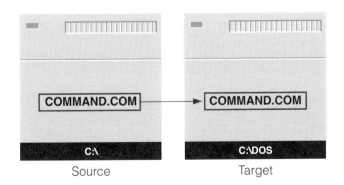

Source   Target

This command copies COMMAND.COM **from** the Root directory (the source), **to** COMMAND.COM in the \DOS directory (the target).

directly to a disk file

Suppose you want to type a quick note to yourself of jobs you must do after lunch. This feature allows you to create a file from your keyboard, and then save it to your disk drive.

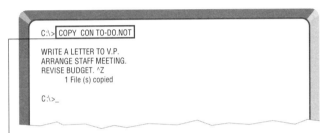

❶ Type **COPY CON TO-DO.NOT** and then press **Enter**.

❷ Type **WRITE A LETTER TO V.P.** Press **Enter**.

   Type **ARRANGE STAFF MEETING.** Press **Enter**.

   Type **REVISE BUDGET.**

❸ Press **F6** or **Ctrl-Z** (displayed on screen as **^Z**) Press **Enter** and the file is copied to the root directory of the C: drive and named TO-DO.NOT.

Note: CON is an abbreviation for Console (also referred to as Keyboard).

RENAME

The Rename command (typed as REN) allows you to change the name of a file or group of files.

Wildcards (* or ?) can be used in either the file name or the extension.

Note: You can only rename files within a directory. Files cannot be renamed across disk drives or directories.

The Rename command is:

REN	FILE SPECIFICATION	NEW FILE NAME AND EXTENSION

FILE SPECIFICATION	Tells DOS the path to the file and its name.
NEW FILE NAME AND EXTENSION	Tells DOS the new name for the file.

RENAME A FILE

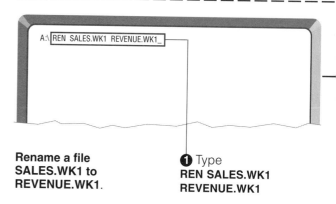

```
A:\ REN SALES.WK1 REVENUE.WK1_
```

Rename a file SALES.WK1 to REVENUE.WK1.

❶ Type **REN SALES.WK1 REVENUE.WK1**

RENAME A FILE USING THE * WILDCARD

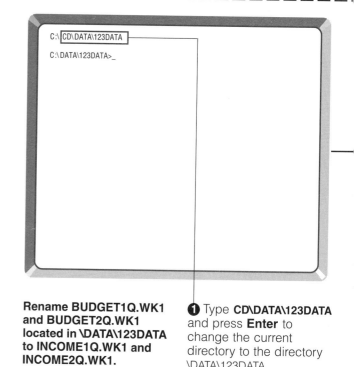

```
C:\ CD\DATA\123DATA
C:\DATA\123DATA>_
```

Rename BUDGET1Q.WK1 and BUDGET2Q.WK1 located in \DATA\123DATA to INCOME1Q.WK1 and INCOME2Q.WK1.

❶ Type **CD\DATA\123DATA** and press **Enter** to change the current directory to the directory \DATA\123DATA.

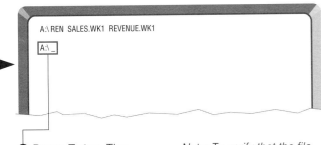

❷ Press **Enter**. The system prompt *"A:\>"* appears, indicating the file has been renamed.

*Note: To verify that the file was renamed correctly, type **DIR** and then press **Enter** to display the new file name and extension.*

GETTING
STARTED

MANAGING
YOUR
DIRECTORIES

**MANAGING
YOUR FILES**

MANAGING
YOUR
DISKETTES

MANAGING
YOUR
HARD DISK

CREATING
BATCH FILES

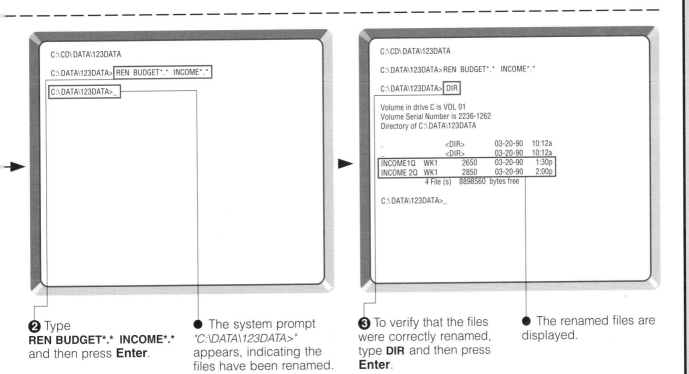

❷ Type **REN BUDGET*.* INCOME*.*** and then press **Enter**.

● The system prompt *"C:\DATA\123DATA>"* appears, indicating the files have been renamed.

❸ To verify that the files were correctly renamed, type **DIR** and then press **Enter**.

● The renamed files are displayed.

ERASE

The Erase command erases files that are no longer required from your hard disk or diskettes.

The Erase command is:

ERASE	FILE SPECIFICATION	/P

FILE SPECIFICATION	Tells DOS the path to the file and its name (example: C:\DATA\123DATA \BUDGET1Q.WK1).
/P	Tells DOS that you want to request verification before erasing each file. The /P parameter only works on DOS Version 4 or higher.

Note: Always change the current drive and directory to the location of the file to be erased. The path can then be omitted from the file specification.

Caution

Once you erase a file, it cannot be retrieved. Use this command with care when erasing single files. If you are erasing files using the * or ? wildcards, use the /P parameter to verify the files to be erased.

ERASE A FILE

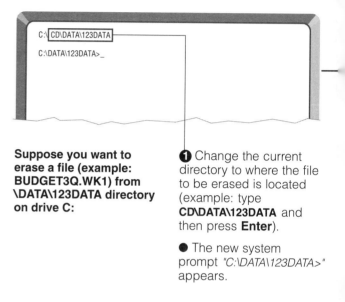

Suppose you want to erase a file (example: BUDGET3Q.WK1) from \DATA\123DATA directory on drive C:

❶ Change the current directory to where the file to be erased is located (example: type **CD\DATA\123DATA** and then press **Enter**).

● The new system prompt *"C:\DATA\123DATA>"* appears.

ERASE MULTIPLE FILES USING THE * WILDCARD

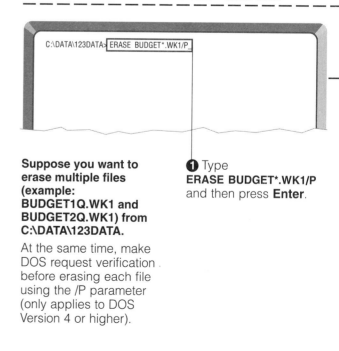

Suppose you want to erase multiple files (example: BUDGET1Q.WK1 and BUDGET2Q.WK1) from C:\DATA\123DATA.

At the same time, make DOS request verification before erasing each file using the /P parameter (only applies to DOS Version 4 or higher).

❶ Type **ERASE BUDGET*.WK1/P** and then press **Enter**.

GETTING
STARTED

MANAGING
YOUR
DIRECTORIES

**MANAGING
YOUR FILES**

MANAGING
YOUR
DISKETTES

MANAGING
YOUR
HARD DISK

CREATING
BATCH FILES

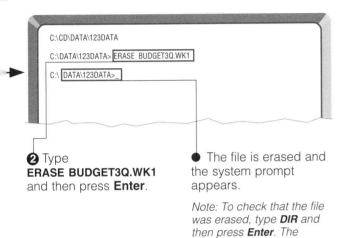

❷ Type
ERASE BUDGET3Q.WK1
and then press **Enter**.

● The file is erased and
the system prompt
appears.

*Note: To check that the file
was erased, type **DIR** and
then press **Enter**. The
directory display will not
include the
BUDGET3Q.WK1 file.*

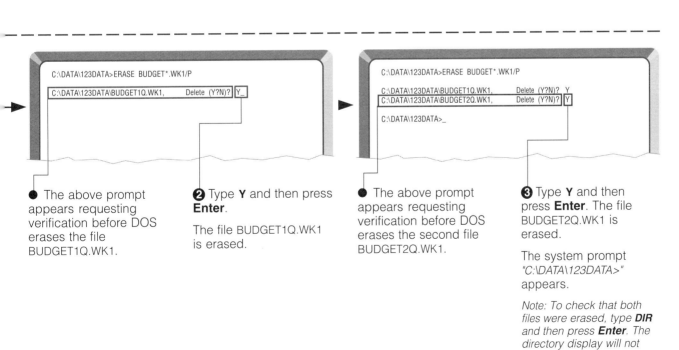

● The above prompt
appears requesting
verification before DOS
erases the file
BUDGET1Q.WK1.

❷ Type **Y** and then press
Enter.

The file BUDGET1Q.WK1
is erased.

● The above prompt
appears requesting
verification before DOS
erases the second file
BUDGET2Q.WK1.

❸ Type **Y** and then
press **Enter**. The file
BUDGET2Q.WK1 is
erased.

The system prompt
"C:\DATA\123DATA>"
appears.

*Note: To check that both
files were erased, type **DIR**
and then press **Enter**. The
directory display will not
include the
BUDGET1Q.WK1 and
BUDGET2Q.WK1 files.*

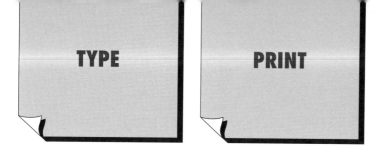

TYPE

The Type command displays the contents of a file on your computer screen. It will work on most files containing text.

Note: If you try to type a DOS or application program file, the screen will be filled with machine code symbols.

The Type command is:

TYPE	FILE SPECIFICATION

FILE SPECIFICATION Tells DOS the drive, directory route, and file name and extension of the file to be displayed on screen.

Note: Always change the current drive and directory to where the file to be typed is located. The path can then be omitted from the file specification.

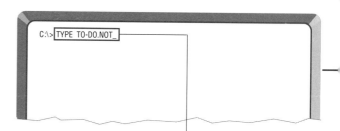

```
C:\> TYPE TO-DO.NOT_
```

Display a text file (example: TO-DO.NOT located in the Root directory) on the screen.

❶ Type **TYPE TO-DO.NOT** and then press **Enter**.

*Note: If the **TO-DO.NOT** file contains more than one screen of text, type **TO-DO.NOT¦MORE** and then press **Enter**. One screen of text is displayed. Press any key to display the next screen of text and so on.*

PRINT

The Print command allows you to print the contents of any text file to the printer.

Since Print is an external command, the Path command should include C:\DOS (refer to page 9). If it does not, the current drive and directory must be changed to C:\DOS before issuing this command.

Note: The path C:\DOS can be automatically specified as part of the AUTOEXEC.BAT file (refer to page 56).

The Print command is:

PRINT	FILE SPECIFICATION

FILE SPECIFICATION Tells DOS the drive, directory route, file name and extension of the file to be printed.

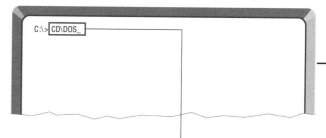

```
C:\> CD\DOS_
```

Print a text file named MEMO.1 located in the subdirectory \DATA\WPDATA.

❶ Type **CD\DOS** and then press **Enter** to change the current directory to the DOS directory.

```
C:\>TYPE TO-DO.NOT

WRITE LETTER TO V.P.
ARRANGE STAFF MEETING.
REVISE BUDGET.

C:\>_
```

● The text in the
TO-DO.NOT file is
displayed.

*Note: To print the contents
of the file directory to the
printer, type*
TYPE TO-DO.NOT>PRN
and then press ***Enter****.*

Print screen

To print the entire screen press [Print Screen] or [Shift] [PrtSc].
Make sure your printer is connected and turned on.

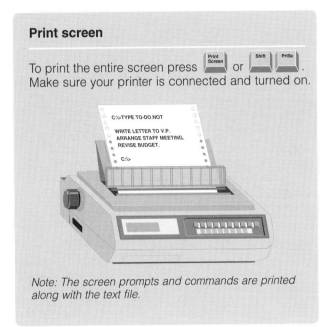

*Note: The screen prompts and commands are printed
along with the text file.*

```
C:\>CD\DOS

C:\DOS> PRINT \DATA\WPDATA\MEMO.1

C:\DATA\PWDATA\MEMO.1 is currently being printed

C:\DOS>_
```

❷ Type **PRINT
\DATA\WPDATA\MEMO.1**
and then press **Enter**.

*Note: Since the text file is
located on the same drive
as the current drive, it can
be omitted from the file
specification.*

*If MEMO.1 is located in the
root directory of drive A:,
type* ***PRINT A:\MEMO.1*** *and
then press* ***Enter****.*

● DOS displays a
message that the file
MEMO.1 is currently
being printed.

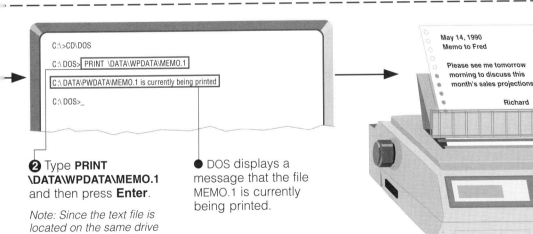

May 14, 1990
Memo to Fred

Please see me tomorrow
morning to discuss this
month's sales projections.

Richard

GETTING
STARTED

MANAGING
YOUR
DIRECTORIES

**MANAGING
YOUR FILES**

MANAGING
YOUR
DISKETTES

MANAGING
YOUR
HARD DISK

CREATING
BATCH FILES

3.5/5.25 INCH DISKETTES

The DOS commands in this chapter work on entire diskettes instead of individual files.

The first IBM microcomputers used 5.25 inch diskettes with only 160 K of memory capacity. As the technology improved, double-sided high capacity diskettes became available with 1200 K or 1.2 MB of memory.

With the release of the IBM PS/2 family of microcomputers, 3.5 inch high capacity, 720 K and 1.44 MB diskettes were added to the line.

Note: K is an abbreviation for Kilobytes (or 1,000 bytes). A byte represents one character.

MB is an abbreviation for Megabytes (or 1,000,000 bytes).

DISKETTE SIZES AND CAPACITY

Size	Capacity	Hardware	DOS Versions
5.25 inch	1.2 MB	IBM AT and compatibles	Version 3 or later
5.25 inch	360 K	IBM PC, PC/XT and compatibles	Version 2 or later
5.25 inch	320 K	IBM PC, PC/XT and compatibles	All Versions
5.25 inch	180 K	IBM PC, PC/XT and compatibles	Version 2 or later
5.25 inch	160 K	IBM PC, PC/XT and compatibles	All Versions
3.5 inch	1.44 MB	IBM PS/2 (not including Model 25)	Version 3.3 or later
3.5 inch	720 K	IBM PS/2 Model 30 and compatibles	Version 3.2 or later

5.25 INCH DISKETTE

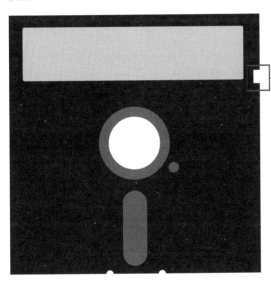

Write protect notch

The open notch on the right side of the diskette lets you copy information to or delete information from the diskette.

By placing a small piece of tape over the notch, the diskette becomes write protected. You can still use the diskette, but you cannot add or delete information to or from it.

Diskettes that do not have a notch are permanently write protected. Many application programs are permanently write protected to guard their files from being deleted or modified.

3.5 INCH DISKETTE

Write protect switch

The switch works similar to the notch on the 5.25 inch diskette. With the switch in the closed position, you can erase, modify or add information to the diskette.

With the switch in the open position, as illustrated to the left, the diskette is write protected.

Note: Make sure your diskettes are properly labeled and protected from extreme heat or cold, humidity, food and drinks.

Keep diskettes away from magnetic influences such as telephones or magnetic paper clip holders.

GETTING STARTED

MANAGING YOUR DIRECTORIES

MANAGING YOUR FILES

MANAGING YOUR DISKETTES

MANAGING YOUR HARD DISK

CREATING BATCH FILES

FORMAT

The Format command prepares a new or previously formatted diskette to have data and program files stored on it. This command also checks for bad sectors on the diskette, and sets up an index that keeps track of information stored on it.

Since Format is an external command, the Path command should include C:\DOS. If it does not, the current drive and directory must be changed to C:\DOS before issuing this command (refer to page 9).

Note: The path C:\DOS can be automatically specified as part of the AUTOEXEC.BAT file (refer to page 56).

The Format command is:

FORMAT   **DRIVE**

DRIVE   Tells DOS the drive you want to format (A: or B:)

Note: **Do not format the C: drive** *unless you have checked with a system specialist.*

Caution

The format command destroys all information on the diskette being formatted. Do not format a diskette containing data you want to retain.

DOS Version 3.1 or earlier

If you type the format command and do not specify a drive, the current drive is formatted. If your system prompt is C:\>, you will erase the entire hard disk.

Note: If you format a 360 K diskette in a high-capacity drive, it can be used in that drive. However, it is not advisable to use that same diskette in a standard 360 K double-sided drive.

FORMAT A DISKETTE AND ADD A VOLUME LABEL

C:\DOS> FORMAT A:_

Format a diskette in drive A: and name it MEMOS. The name MEMOS is called a Volume label.

Note: This label is used to identify the disk .

❶ Type **CD\DOS** and then press **Enter** to change the current directory to the \DOS directory.

❷ Type **FORMAT A:**

Note: DOS Version 4 lets you add the Volume label at this point (example: type **FORMAT A:/V:MEMOS***).*

Add system startup files to diskette

To add the system startup files while formatting the diskette, type **FORMAT A:/S**. You can then start DOS directly from the diskette. Adding the **/S** option reduces the storage capacity of the diskette by up to 100 K, depending on the DOS Version.

GETTING
STARTED

MANAGING
YOUR
DIRECTORIES

MANAGING
YOUR FILES

**MANAGING
YOUR
DISKETTES**

MANAGING
YOUR
HARD DISK

CREATING
BATCH FILES

```
C:\DOS>FORMAT A:
Insert new diskette for drive A:
and press ENTER when ready . . .

XX percent of disk formatted
```

```
C:\DOS>FORMAT A:
Insert new diskette for drive A:
and press ENTER when ready . . .

Format complete

Volume label (11 characters, ENTER for none) ? MEMOS_
```

❸ Press **Enter** and the prompt above appears.

❹ Insert the diskette to be formatted in drive A: and then press **Enter**.

● DOS reports its progress with the message displayed above.

Note: For earlier DOS versions the message is ...Formatting or Head: 0 Cylinder: 0 (the numbers change as the diskette is formatted).

● The above message appears when the diskette is formatted.

❺ Type the Volume label (example: **MEMOS**) and then press **Enter**. If no Volume lable is required, just press **Enter**.

Note: The label can contain up to 11 characters including one blank space. Permissible characters are letters A to Z, digits 0 through 9 and $ – ( ) _ { } #.

To view the Volume label

```
A:\>VOL

Volume in drive A is MEMOS
Volume Serial number is 1E19-0FF0

A:\>_
```

❶ Type **VOL** and then press **Enter**.

```
C:\DOS>FORMAT A:
Insert new diskette for drive A:
and press ENTER when ready . . .

Format complete

Volume label (11 characters, ENTER for none) ? MEMOS

    1457664    bytes total disk space
      53760    bytes in bad sectors
    1403904    bytes available on disk

        512    bytes in each allocation unit
       2847    allocation units available on disk

Volume Serial Number is 1E19–0FF0

Format another (Y/N) ?
```

● DOS then tells you the total capacity of the diskette, unusable bytes in bad sectors, and bytes for storing new data.

Note: Do not use a diskette with bad sectors. This diskette has bad sectors and should not be used. If the diskette is OK, the "bytes in bad sectors" line will not appear.

❻ DOS asks you if you want to format another diskette:

– Type **Y** and then press **Enter** to format another disk.

– Type **N** and then press **Enter** to return to the system prompt.

FORMAT

FORMAT A DISKETTE USING THE F:<SIZE> PARAMETER (DOS VERSION 4 ONLY)

Using the F:<size> parameter, 3.5 and 5.25 inch diskettes can be formatted to any appropriate size from 160 K to 1.44 MB. This is a very useful feature when you are sharing information with a machine that has a lower density drive.

Note: Do not format a diskette to a size greater than its guaranteed capacity.

Diskette Physical Size	Diskette Capacity	Type F:<size>
5.25"	160 K	160
5.25"	180 K	180
5.25"	320 K	320
5.25"	360 K	360
3.5"	720 K	720
5.25"	1.2 MB	1200
3.5"	1.44 MB	1440

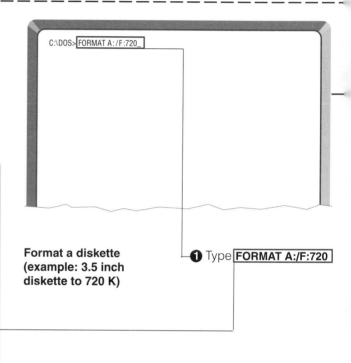

C:\DOS> FORMAT A:/F:720_

Format a diskette (example: 3.5 inch diskette to 720 K)

❶ Type FORMAT A:/F:720

```
C:\>FORMAT A:/F:720
Insert new diskette for drive A:
and press ENTER when ready . . .

XX percent of disk formatted
```

```
C:\>FORMAT A:/F:720
Insert new diskette for drive A:
and press ENTER when ready . . .

Format complete

Volume label (11 characters, ENTER for none)?_
```

2 Press **Enter** and the above prompt appears.

3 Insert the diskette to be formatted in drive A: and press **Enter**.

● DOS reports its progress with the message displayed above.

4 The above message appears when the diskette is formatted.

5 Type a Volume label and then press **Enter**. If no Volume label is required, just press **Enter**.

```
C:\DOS>FORMAT A:/F:720
Insert new diskette for drive A:
and press ENTER when ready . . .

Format complete

Volume label (11 characters, ENTER for none) ?

    730112   bytes total disk space
    730112   bytes available on disk

      1024   bytes in each allocation unit
       713   allocation units available on disk

Volume Serial Number is 2A17-17EF

Format another (Y/N) ?_
```

● DOS then tells you the total capacity of the diskette and bytes for storing new data.

6 DOS asks you if you want to format another diskette:

– Type **Y** and then press **Enter** to format another disk.

– Type **N** and then press **Enter** to return to the DOS system prompt.

GETTING
STARTED

MANAGING
YOUR
DIRECTORIES

MANAGING
YOUR FILES

**MANAGING
YOUR
DISKETTES**

MANAGING
YOUR
HARD DISK

CREATING
BATCH FILES

DISKCOPY

The Diskcopy command is used to copy the entire contents of one diskette to another diskette, so that the second diskette is an exact copy of the first. This command only works on diskettes of the same size and capacity.

Since Diskcopy is an external command, the Path command should include C:\DOS. If it does not, the current drive and directory must be changed to C:\DOS before issuing this command (refer to page 9).

Note: The path C:\DOS can be automatically specified as part of the AUTOEXEC.BAT file (refer to page 56).

The Diskcopy command is:

DISKCOPY	SOURCE DRIVE	TARGET DRIVE

SOURCE DRIVE   Tells DOS the drive **from** which the files are to be copied.

TARGET DRIVE   Tells DOS the drive **to** which the files are to be copied.

Caution

The Diskcopy command automatically formats the target diskette during the copy process. Make sure the target diskette does not contain any files that you want to keep.

DISKCOPY USING ONE DRIVE

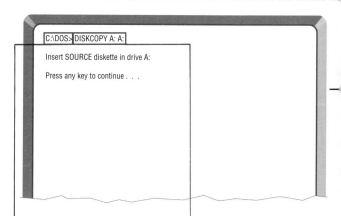

❶ Type **CD\DOS** and then press **Enter** to change the current directory to the \DOS directory.

❷ Type **DISKCOPY A: A:** and then press **Enter**.

❸ Insert the SOURCE diskette into drive A: and then press any key.

DISKCOPY USING TWO DRIVES

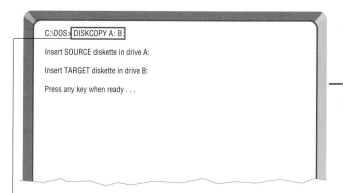

❶ Type **DISKCOPY A: B:** and then press **Enter**.

❷ Insert the SOURCE diskette in drive A: and the TARGET diskette in drive B: and then press any key.

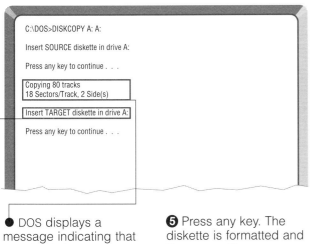

```
C:\DOS>DISKCOPY A: A:

Insert SOURCE diskette in drive A:

Press any key to continue . . .

Copying 80 tracks
18 Sectors/Track, 2 Side(s)

Insert TARGET diskette in drive A:

Press any key to continue . . .
```

● DOS displays a message indicating that copying is in progress.

❹ Insert the TARGET diskette in drive A: when requested by DOS.

❺ Press any key. The diskette is formatted and then some files are copied onto it. The machine will ask you to switch diskettes several times to copy the remaining files.

```
C:\DOS>DISKCOPY A: A:

Insert SOURCE diskette in drive A:

Press any key to continue . . .

Copying 80 tracks
18 Sectors/Track, 2 Side(s)

Insert TARGET diskette in drive A:

Press any key to continue . . .

Volume Serial Number is 1FF5-1752

Copy another diskette (Y/N)? _
```

● DOS displays a message indicating that the DISKCOPY is complete.

❻ DOS asks you if you want to copy another diskette:

– Type **Y** and then press **Enter** to copy another disk.

– Type **N** and then press **Enter** to return to the system prompt.

```
C:\DOS>DISKCOPY A: B:

Insert SOURCE diskette in drive A:

Insert TARGET diskette in drive B:

Press any key when ready . . .

Copying 80 tracks
18 Sectors/Track, 2 Side(s)

Volume Serial Number is 1FF9-2D2B

Copy another diskette (Y/N)? □
```

● DOS displays a message indicating that copying is in progress followed by a message that the DISKCOPY is complete.

❸ DOS asks you if you want to copy another diskette:

– Type **Y** and then press **Enter** to copy another disk.

– Type **N** and then press **Enter** to return to the system prompt.

GETTING STARTED

MANAGING YOUR DIRECTORIES

MANAGING YOUR FILES

MANAGING YOUR DISKETTES

MANAGING YOUR HARD DISK

CREATING BATCH FILES

BACKUP

The Backup command copies data files on your hard disk to backup diskettes. This protects your data in case of a catastrophic failure of your hard disk or accidental erasure of important files.

Backup your data files regularly (daily or weekly).

The complete Backup procedure consists of two commands—Backup and Restore. The Backup command is described on these two pages. The Restore command is described on the next two pages.

Since Backup and Restore are external commands, the Path command should include C:\DOS. If it does not, the current drive and directory must be changed to C:\DOS before issuing these commands (refer to page 9).

Note: The path C:\DOS can be automatically specified as part of the AUTOEXEC.BAT file (refer to page 56).

The Backup command is:

BACKUP	SOURCE FILE SPECIFICATION	TARGET DRIVE	/S	/F

SOURCE FILE SPECIFICATION	Tells DOS the drive, directory route, and file name and extension of the files to be backed up.
TARGET DRIVE	Tells DOS the drive to which the files are to be backed up.
/S	Tells DOS to backup files in all subdirectories below the directory specified in the source file specification.
/F	Tells DOS to format the target diskette if it is not already formatted.

Note: If you do not specify a file name and extension, DOS uses *.* as the default file name and extension.

EXAMPLE:

Backup all files and directories starting from the \DATA directory to a series of diskettes. The number of diskettes required depends on the total size of the files to be backed up and the size of the diskettes used.

Backup diskettes required

To backup 5,500 K of data files with 720 K diskettes requires $5,500 \div 720 = 8$ diskettes.

Note: Since you already have the original program and DOS diskettes, these files are not normally backed up using this command.

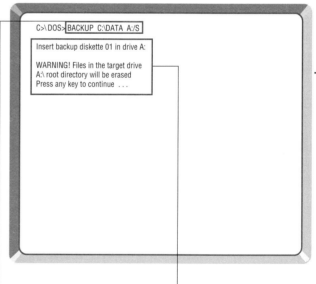

❶ Type
BACKUP C:\DATA A:/S
and then press **Enter**.

Note: If \DATA is not specified, DOS backs up files from the current directory (or \DOS in this example).

❷ Insert Backup diskette **01** in drive A: and then press any key.

GETTING
STARTED

MANAGING
YOUR
DIRECTORIES

MANAGING
YOUR FILES

MANAGING
YOUR
DISKETTES

**MANAGING
YOUR
HARD DISK**

CREATING
BATCH FILES

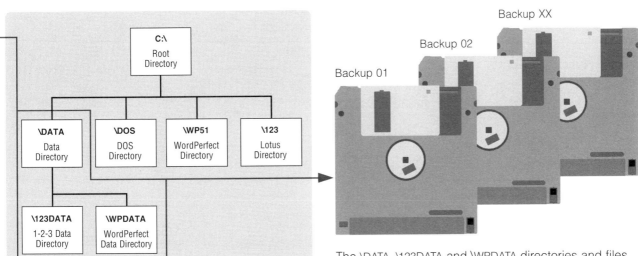

```
C:\
Root
Directory

\DATA          \DOS           \WP51          \123
Data           DOS            WordPerfect    Lotus
Directory      Directory      Directory      Directory

\123DATA       \WPDATA
1-2-3 Data     WordPerfect
Directory      Data Directory
```

Backup 01   Backup 02   Backup XX

The \DATA, \123DATA and \WPDATA directories and files
are copied to backup diskettes 01 to XX.

```
C>\DOS>BACKUP C:\DATA A:/S

Insert backup diskette 01 in drive A:

WARNING! Files in the target drive
A:\ root directory will be erased
Press any key to continue . . .

*** Backing up files to drive A:  ***
Diskette Number: 01

\DATA\123DATA\REVENUE.WK1
\DATA\123DATA\INCOME1Q.WK1
\DATA\123DATA\INCOME2Q.WK1
\DATA\123DATA\INCOME3Q.WK1
\DATA\123DATA\PROJECT1.WK1
\DATA\123DATA\PROJECT2.WK1
\DATA\123DATA\INCOME4Q.WK1
\DATA\123DATA\SALES1Q.WK1_
```

```
\DATA\123DATA\SALES2Q.WK1
\DATA\123DATA\SALES3Q.WK1
\DATA\123DATA\SALES4Q.WK1
\DATA\WPDATA\MERGE.LET

Insert backup diskette 02 in drive A:

WARNING! Files in the target dirve
A:\ root directory will be erased
Press any key to continue . . .

\DATA\WPDATA\PRIMARY.LET
\DATA\WPDATA\DO-MON.MEM
\DATA\WPDATA\DO-TUE.MEM
\DATA\WPDATA\BUDGET1Q.LET
\DATA\WPDATA\BUDGET2Q.LET
\DATA\WPDATA\BUDGET3Q.LET
\DATA\WPDATA\BUDGET4Q.LET
\DATA\WPDATA\JIM-R1.TXT
\DATA\WPDATA\JIM-R2.TXT
\DATA\WPDATA\JIM-R3.TXT

C:\DOS>_
```

● DOS begins backing
up files to diskette **01** in
drive A:.

❸ Remove Backup
diskette **01**. Insert Backup
diskette **02** in drive A: and
then press any key.

● The remaining files are
backed up to diskette **02**
in drive A:. When the
"C:\DOS" prompt appears,
all files are backed up.

*Note: More than two backup
diskettes may be required.*

RESTORE

The Restore command is used to restore data files on backup diskettes to your hard drive.

Files duplicated using the Backup command can only be accessed with the Restore command.

The Restore command is:

RESTORE	SOURCE DRIVE	SOURCE FILE SPECIFICATION	/S

SOURCE DRIVE
Tells DOS the drive containing the backup diskettes.

SOURCE FILE SPECIFICATION
Tells DOS the drive, directory route, file name and extension to where the files are to be restored.

/S
Tells DOS to restore files to all subdirectories.

Caution

Always use the same Version of DOS for both the Backup and Restore commands. This is critical when you are restoring files to another hard drive.

EXAMPLE:

Restore all files and directories on backup diskettes to the hard drive \DATA directory.

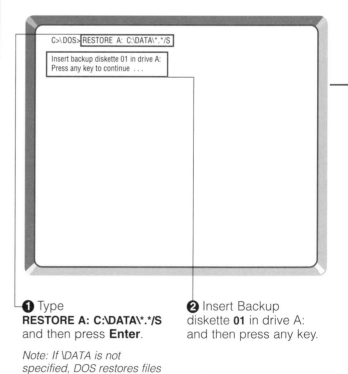

```
C>\DOS> RESTORE A: C:\DATA\*.*/S

Insert backup diskette 01 in drive A:
Press any key to continue . . .
```

1 Type
RESTORE A: C:\DATA*.*/S and then press **Enter**.

Note: If \DATA is not specified, DOS restores files to the current directory (or \DOS in this example).

2 Insert Backup diskette **01** in drive A: and then press any key.

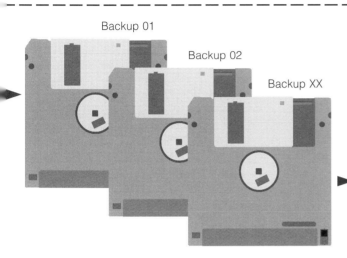

Backup 01

Backup 02

Backup XX

All files and directories on the backup diskettes are copied to the hard drive \DATA, \123DATA and \WPDATA directories.

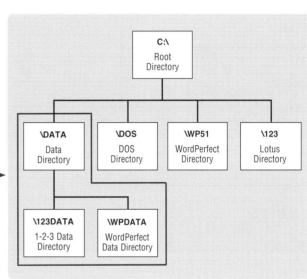

```
                              ┌──────────┐
                              │   C:\    │
                              │  Root    │
                              │ Directory│
                              └──────────┘
    ┌──────────┬──────────┬──────────┬──────────┐
┌─────────┐ ┌─────────┐ ┌─────────┐ ┌─────────┐
│ \DATA   │ │ \DOS    │ │ \WP51   │ │ \123    │
│ Data    │ │ DOS     │ │WordPerfect│ Lotus   │
│Directory│ │Directory│ │Directory│ │Directory│
└─────────┘ └─────────┘ └─────────┘ └─────────┘
┌─────────┐ ┌─────────┐
│\123DATA │ │ \WPDATA │
│1-2-3 Data│ │WordPerfect│
│Directory│ │Data Directory│
└─────────┘ └─────────┘
```

```
C>\DOS>RESTORE  A:  C:\DATA\*.*/S

Insert backup diskette 01 in drive A:
Press any key to continue . . .

*** Files were backed up 05-11-90 ***

*** Restoring files from drive A:  ***
Diskette Number: 01
\DATA\123DATA\REVENUE.WK1
\DATA\123DATA\INCOME1Q.WK1
\DATA\123DATA\INCOME2Q.WK1
\DATA\123DATA\INCOME3Q.WK1
\DATA\123DATA\PROJECT1.WK1
\DATA\123DATA\PROJECT2.WK1
\DATA\123DATA\INCOME4Q.WK1
\DATA\123DATA\SALES1Q.WK1
\DATA\123DATA\SALES2Q.WK1
\DATA\123DATA\SALES3Q.WK1_
```

```
\DATA\123DATA\SALES4Q.WK1
\DATA\WPDATA\MERGE.LET

Insert backup diskette 02 in drive A:
Press any key to continue . . .

*** Restoring files from drive A: ***
Diskette: 02
\DATA\WPDATA\PRIMARY.LET
\DATA\WPDATA\DO-MON.MEM
\DATA\WPDATA\DO-TUE.MEM
\DATA\WPDATA\BUDGET1Q.LET
\DATA\WPDATA\BUDGET2Q.LET
\DATA\WPDATA\BUDGET3Q.LET
\DATA\WPDATA\BUDGET4Q.LET
\DATA\WPDATA\JIM-R1.TXT
\DATA\WPDATA\JIM-R2.TXT
\DATA\WPDATA\JIM-R3.TXT

C:\DOS>_
```

● DOS begins restoring files to the hard drive \DATA directory.

❸ Remove Backup diskette **01**. Insert Backup diskette **02** in drive A: and then press any key.

● Continue following the prompts until the remaining files are restored to the hard drive \DATA directory.

XCOPY

The Xcopy command copies files and directories, including lower level subdirectories, from a hard disk to a diskette or vice versa.

The Copy command can only copy files. It cannot copy directories.

Since Xcopy is an external command, the Path command should include C:\DOS. If it does not, the current drive and directory must be changed to C:\DOS before issuing this command (refer to page 9).

Note: The path C:\DOS can be automatically specified as part of the AUTOEXEC.BAT file (refer to page 56).

The Xcopy command is:

XCOPY	SOURCE FILE SPECIFICATION	TARGET PATH	/S

SOURCE FILE SPECIFICATION	Tells DOS the drive, directory route, file name and extension of the files to be copied.
TARGET PATH	Tells DOS the drive and directory to which the files are to be copied.
/S	Tells DOS to copy all directories and files.

*Note: If you do not specify a file name and extension, XCOPY uses *.* as the default file name and extension.*

EXAMPLE:

Copy all files and directories starting from the C:\DATA directory on to diskette A:

Then copy the files from diskette A: to another hard drive.

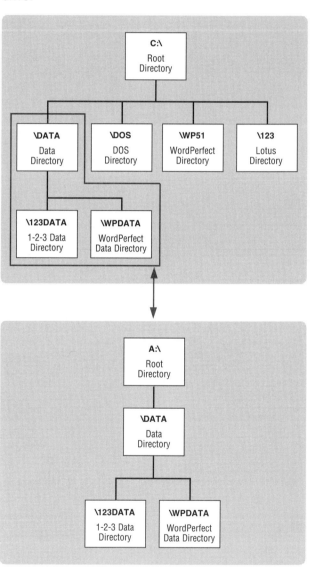

Note: XCOPY should only be used when the size of the files to be copied are less than the capacity of one diskette.

GETTING
STARTED

MANAGING
YOUR
DIRECTORIES

MANAGING
YOUR FILES

MANAGING
YOUR
DISKETTES

**MANAGING
YOUR
HARD DISK**

CREATING
BATCH FILES

COPY FILES AND DIRECTORIES FROM A HARD DISK TO A DISKETTE

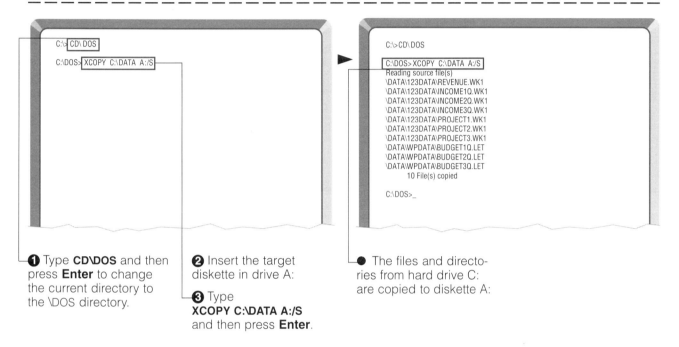

C:\> CD\DOS

C:\DOS> XCOPY C:\DATA A:/S

C:\>CD\DOS

C:\DOS>XCOPY C:\DATA A:/S
Reading source file(s)
\DATA\123DATA\REVENUE.WK1
\DATA\123DATA\INCOME1Q.WK1
\DATA\123DATA\INCOME2Q.WK1
\DATA\123DATA\INCOME3Q.WK1
\DATA\123DATA\PROJECT1.WK1
\DATA\123DATA\PROJECT2.WK1
\DATA\123DATA\PROJECT3.WK1
\DATA\WPDATA\BUDGET1Q.LET
\DATA\WPDATA\BUDGET2Q.LET
\DATA\WPDATA\BUDGET3Q.LET
        10 File(s) copied

C:\DOS>_

1 Type **CD\DOS** and then press **Enter** to change the current directory to the \DOS directory.

2 Insert the target diskette in drive A:

3 Type **XCOPY C:\DATA A:/S** and then press **Enter**.

● The files and directories from hard drive C: are copied to diskette A:

COPY FILES AND DIRECTORIES FROM A DISKETTE TO A HARD DISK

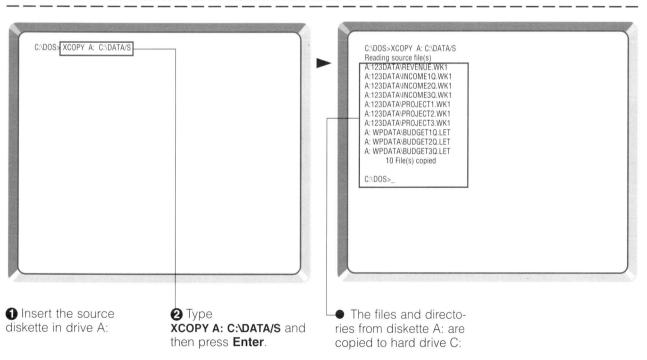

C:\DOS> XCOPY A: C:\DATA/S

C:\DOS>XCOPY A: C:\DATA/S
Reading source file(s)
A:123DATA\REVENUE.WK1
A:123DATA\INCOME1Q.WK1
A:123DATA\INCOME2Q.WK1
A:123DATA\INCOME3Q.WK1
A:123DATA\PROJECT1.WK1
A:123DATA\PROJECT2.WK1
A:123DATA\PROJECT3.WK1
A: WPDATA\BUDGET1Q.LET
A: WPDATA\BUDGET2Q.LET
A: WPDATA\BUDGET3Q.LET
        10 File(s) copied

C:\DOS>_

1 Insert the source diskette in drive A:

2 Type **XCOPY A: C:\DATA/S** and then press **Enter**.

● The files and directories from diskette A: are copied to hard drive C:

CHECK DISK

The Check Disk command (typed as CHKDSK) is used to display the status of files and directories on a hard disk or diskette. It also displays the computer's electronic (or RAM) memory up to 640 K and how much is available for running programs.

As a disk fills up, files are separated into units and given allocation identification numbers. A File Allocation Table keeps track of all the allocation units.

System or program problems can cause the table to lose track of some of these units, which are then called "open" files.

Check Disk identifies that "open" files exist. It does not try to recover them unless you have specified the /F parameter.

Since Check Disk is an external command, the Path command should include C:\DOS. If it does not, the current drive and directory must be changed to C:\DOS before issuing this command (refer to page 9).

Note: The path C:\DOS can be automatically specified as part of the AUTOEXEC.BAT file (refer to page 56).

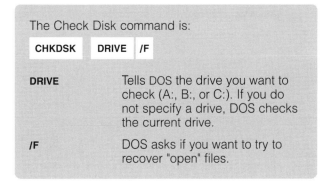

The Check Disk command is:

CHKDSK	DRIVE	/F

DRIVE	Tells DOS the drive you want to check (A:, B:, or C:). If you do not specify a drive, DOS checks the current drive.
/F	DOS asks if you want to try to recover "open" files.

CHECK DISK AND MEMORY STATUS

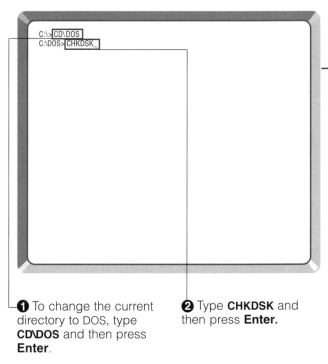

❶ To change the current directory to DOS, type **CD\DOS** and then press **Enter**.

❷ Type **CHKDSK** and then press **Enter.**

FIX ERRORS ON THE DISK (/F PARAMETER)

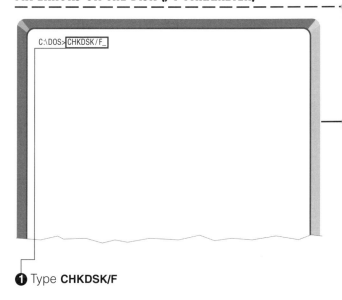

❶ Type **CHKDSK/F**

GETTING
STARTED

MANAGING
YOUR
DIRECTORIES

MANAGING
YOUR FILES

MANAGING
YOUR
DISKETTES

MANAGING
YOUR
HARD DISK

CREATING
BATCH FILES

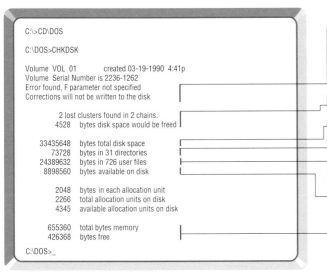

```
C:\>CD\DOS

C:\DOS>CHKDSK

Volume VOL 01        created 03-19-1990 4:41p
Volume Serial Number is 2236-1262
Error found, F parameter not specified
Corrections will not be written to the disk

        2 lost clusters found in 2 chains.
     4528    bytes disk space would be freed

 33435648    bytes total disk space
    73728    bytes in 31 directories
 24389632    bytes in 726 user files
  8898560    bytes available on disk

     2048    bytes in each allocation unit
     2266    total allocation units on disk
     4345    available allocation units on disk

   655360    total bytes memory
   426368    bytes free

C:\DOS>_
```

These lines tell you that there are errors in the File Allocation Table. To fix the errors use the /F parameter described below. If no errors exist, these lines do not appear.

The amount of disk space occupied by open files.

The total amount of storage space on the disk.

The amount of memory occupied by the directories.

The number of programs and data files and the space they occupy.

The amount of disk space still available.

These lines tell you how much memory the computer has and how much of it is available for running programs.

● DOS displays the disk and computer memory status.

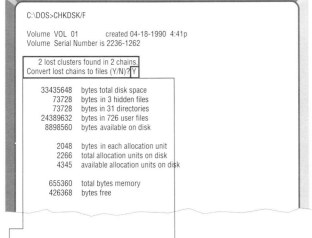

```
C:\DOS>CHKDSK/F

Volume VOL 01        created 04-18-1990 4:41p
Volume Serial Number is 2236-1262

    2 lost clusters found in 2 chains.
Convert lost chains to files (Y/N)? Y

 33435648    bytes total disk space
    73728    bytes in 3 hidden files
    73728    bytes in 31 directories
 24389632    bytes in 726 user files
  8898560    bytes available on disk

     2048    bytes in each allocation unit
     2266    total allocation units on disk
     4345    available allocation units on disk

   655360    total bytes memory
   426368    bytes free
```

Note: If you typed **Y** in Step 3, DOS converts the "open" files into files named FILE0001.CHK, FILE0002.CHK, etc.

These files are saved to the root directory. You can use the Type command to display their contents. If the files contain useful information, they should be kept.

However, if the information is of no value, delete the files to increase the storage capacity on your hard disk.

❷ Press **Enter** and DOS displays the message above if "open" files are detected.

❸ Type **Y** and then press **Enter** to fix the errors in the File Allocation Table.

or

Type **N** and then press **Enter** to fix the disk, but not save the contents of the lost allocation units.

CREATE A BATCH FILE

After working with DOS for a period of time, you will find yourself typing similar sequences of DOS commands on a regular basis to perform common tasks.

To automate and speed up the way you use DOS, the program allows you to package these frequently used command sequences into special files called "batch files".

To issue a group of commands in a batch file, type the file name (not the extension) and press Enter to run all the commands it contains.

You can create as many batch files as you like to automate your work.

Naming batch files

Do not give a batch file the same file name as a DOS internal or external command.

CREATE A BATCH FILE TO DISPLAY THE \123DATA DIRECTORY SORTED BY FILE SIZE IN DESCENDING ORDER

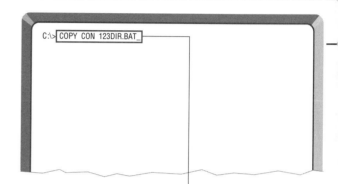

```
C:\> COPY CON 123DIR.BAT_
```

This batch file is useful when you are reviewing a directory to identify old or infrequently used files that you may wish to erase (or delete).

❶ Type COPY CON 123DIR.BAT and then press **Enter**.

Note: The COPY CON command permits you to create and name a text file from the keyboard (refer to page 31).

The batch file must contain the file extension .BAT.

CREATE A
BATCH FILE

CREATE AN
AUTOEXEC.BAT
FILE

GETTING
STARTED

MANAGING
YOUR
DIRECTORIES

MANAGING
YOUR FILES

MANAGING
YOUR
DISKETTES

MANAGING
YOUR
HARD DISK

CREATING
BATCH FILES

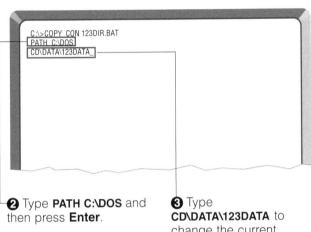

2 Type **PATH C:\DOS** and then press **Enter**.

Note: The Path command C:\DOS allows you to issue external DOS commands such as the Sort command from any directory. Refer to page 9 for a full description of the Path command.

3 Type **CD\DATA\123DATA** to change the current directory to the \DATA\123DATA directory.

4 Type **DIR/P!SORT/R/+16** to display the 123DATA directory, pause every screen, and sort by file size in descending order.

Note: Refer to page 26 for a full description of the Sort command.

5 Press **F6** or **Ctrl-Z** (displayed as ^Z) and then press **Enter**. DOS displays the *"1 File(s) copied"* message.

DISPLAY THE \123DATA DIRECTORY SORTED BY FILE SIZE IN DESCENDING ORDER

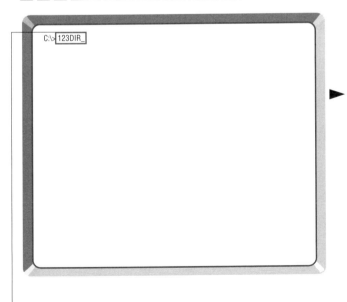

1 Type **123DIR** (the name of the batch file).

Note: To execute a batch file, only type the file name.

2 Press **Enter** and the 123DATA directory is displayed by file size in descending order.

CREATE AN AUTOEXEC.BAT FILE

When you start your computer, DOS searches the root directory of the default drive (usually A:). If the A: drive is empty, DOS proceeds to search the root directory of drive C:.

If DOS finds a file named AUTOEXEC.BAT, it runs this file immediately—bypassing the date and time prompts.

The AUTOEXEC.BAT file allows you full control over the settings and tasks the computer executes each time it starts.

Most computers contain a battery that keeps the correct date and time once they are initially set. The battery maintains the correct date and time even when the power switch is off.

For older computers that do not use a battery, include the date and time commands in your AUTOEXEC.BAT file.

Check to verify if an AUTOEXEC.BAT file exists

Type **CD** to change the current directory to the root directory. Type **DIR AUTOEXEC.BAT** and then press **Enter**. If the file exists, DOS will display it.

If the file does not exist, DOS will report *"File not found"*.

Note: If an AUTOEXEC.BAT file exists and you create a new one using the example that follows—the new AUTOEXEC.BAT file will erase the original file.

Backup existing AUTOEXEC.BAT file

Until you are satisfied that your new AUTOEXEC.BAT file is exactly what you want, retain a copy of the old file.

To change the name of the existing file, type **REN AUTOEXEC.BAT AUTOEXEC.OLD** and then press **Enter**.

CREATE A TYPICAL AUTOEXEC.BAT FILE

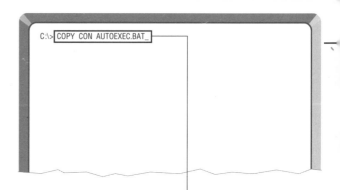

The AUTOEXEC.BAT file created in this example has the following features:

● Allows you to execute DOS external commands, and start 1-2-3 and WordPerfect 5.1 from any drive or directory.

● Sets the system prompt to display the current drive and directory.

● Changes the current directory to \DATA\123DATA. This is the directory containing the 1-2-3 data files.

● Displays the directory of \DATA\123DATA, pauses every screen, and sorts the file names alphabetically in descending order.

❶ Type

COPY CON AUTOEXEC.BAT and then press **Enter** to name and begin the process of creating the AUTOEXEC.BAT file.

GETTING
STARTED

MANAGING
YOUR
DIRECTORIES

MANAGING
YOUR FILES

MANAGING
YOUR
DISKETTES

MANAGING
YOUR
HARD DISK

**CREATING
BATCH FILES**

```
C:\>COPY CON AUTOEXEC.BAT
PATH C:\DOS;C:\123;C:\WP51_
```

```
C:\>COPY CON AUTOEXEC.BAT
PATH C:\DOS;C:\123;C:\WP51
PROMPT $P$G_
```

❷ Type
PATH C:\DOS;C:\123;C:\WP51
and then press **Enter**.

*Note: Since the directories are
specified in the Path command,
you can execute DOS,
Lotus 1-2-3 and WordPerfect
commands (files with EXE,
COM, or BAT extensions) from
any drive or directory.*

❸ Type **PROMPT PG**
and then press **Enter**.

*Note: The Prompt command
customizes the system
prompt. In this example, the
prompt PG changes the
system prompt to display
the current directory of the
current drive.*

If you type	You will get this prompt
Prompt $Q	=
Prompt $$	$
Prompt $T	The current time.
Prompt $D	The current date.
Prompt $P	The current directory of the current drive.
Prompt $V	The DOS version number.
Prompt $N	The default drive.
Prompt $G	>
Prompt $L	<

continued on next page...

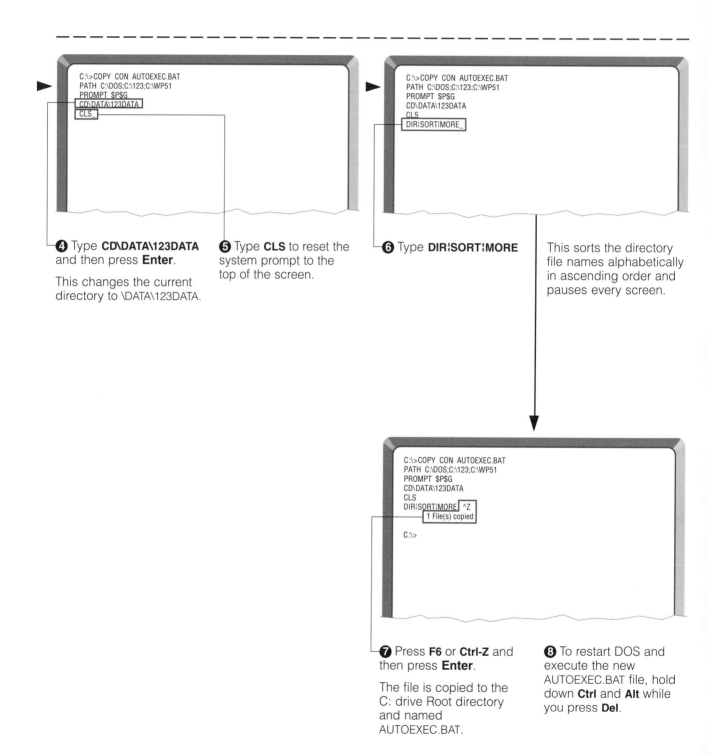

```
C:\>COPY CON AUTOEXEC.BAT
PATH C:\DOS;C:\123;C:\WP51
PROMPT $P$G
CD\DATA\123DATA
CLS_
```

```
C:\>COPY CON AUTOEXEC.BAT
PATH C:\DOS;C:\123;C:\WP51
PROMPT $P$G
CD\DATA\123DATA
CLS
DIR¦SORT¦MORE_
```

4 Type **CD\DATA\123DATA** and then press **Enter**.

This changes the current directory to \DATA\123DATA.

5 Type **CLS** to reset the system prompt to the top of the screen.

6 Type **DIR¦SORT¦MORE**

This sorts the directory file names alphabetically in ascending order and pauses every screen.

```
C:\>COPY CON AUTOEXEC.BAT
PATH C:\DOS;C:\123;C:\WP51
PROMPT $P$G
CD\DATA\123DATA
CLS
DIR¦SORT¦MORE ^Z
                 1 File(s) copied

C:\>
```

7 Press **F6** or **Ctrl-Z** and then press **Enter**.

The file is copied to the C: drive Root directory and named AUTOEXEC.BAT.

8 To restart DOS and execute the new AUTOEXEC.BAT file, hold down **Ctrl** and **Alt** while you press **Del**.

...continued from previous page

DISPLAY THE CONTENTS OF THE AUTOEXEC.BAT FILE

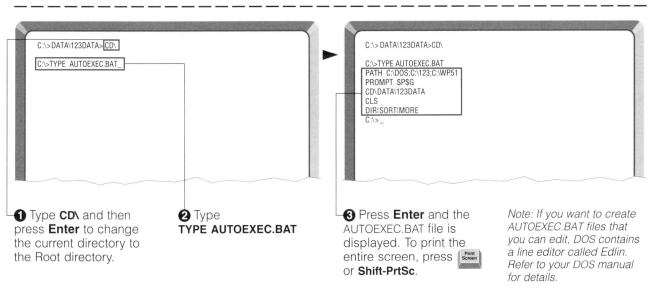

1 Type **CD** and then press **Enter** to change the current directory to the Root directory.

2 Type
TYPE AUTOEXEC.BAT

3 Press **Enter** and the AUTOEXEC.BAT file is displayed. To print the entire screen, press [Print Screen] or **Shift-PrtSc**.

Note: If you want to create AUTOEXEC.BAT files that you can edit, DOS contains a line editor called Edlin. Refer to your DOS manual for details.

GETTING
STARTED

MANAGING
YOUR
DIRECTORIES

MANAGING
YOUR FILES

MANAGING
YOUR
DISKETTES

MANAGING
YOUR
HARD DISK

CREATING
BATCH FILES

GLOSSARY

APPLICATION PROGRAM

A program designed to perform a specific type of work, such as word processing or spreadsheet analysis.

ASCII

ASCII stands for American Standard Code for Information Interchange. It is an industry standard coding scheme using numeric values to represent letters, numbers and symbols.

AUTOEXEC.BAT

A special batch file containing startup commands that DOS performs each time the computer is turned on.

BATCH FILE

A file containing DOS commands. The extension of a batch file is always .BAT. When you type the batch file name at the system prompt, DOS executes the commands in the file.

BOOT

A term used to describe the process of starting up the computer. A cold boot starts the computer from power off and tests all its devices and memory. A warm boot (Ctrl-Alt-Del) restarts the machine when it is on. This is a faster method, because it goes through the startup procedure without turning the power off/on and testing all its devices and memory again.

BYTE

Byte is a term used to measure computer memory and data storage. One byte can store a single computer character (example: a number, letter, or punctuation mark).

COMMAND

A command includes instructions to tell the computer what to do.

COMMAND FILE

A file containing instructions needed to execute a command. If the command file ends in COM or EXE, it executes machine instructions. If the command file ends in BAT, it is a batch file containing DOS commands.

CPU

The part of the computer that calculates, manipulates and processes information. CPU stands for Central Processing Unit.

CURRENT DIRECTORY

DOS searches for files in this directory, unless otherwise instructed.

CURRENT DRIVE

DOS searches for files in this drive, unless otherwise instructed.

DATA

The numbers and text processed by the computer program.

DATA FILE

A file that stores text and numbers used by the computer program.

DIRECTORY

A directory can be compared to a file folder within a cabinet. Directories are used to organize files on a diskette or hard disk.

DISK

A magnetically coated plastic or metal platter used to store information. Disk is a general term that refers to either a diskette or hard disk.

DISK DRIVE

A device that records and plays back information by rotating a disk encoded with magnetic data.

EDIT

The process of adding, deleting or changing information contained in a file.

EXTENDED MEMORY

Additional RAM memory may be added to machines by purchasing appropriate hardware. Some application programs use this extra memory to work more efficiently.

FILE

A file can be compared to a document that contains information.

FILE NAME

DOS uses the file name to locate a file on a disk. The file name consists of eight characters. It can be followed by an extension, which includes a period and up to three additional characters.

FILE SPECIFICATION

A file is specified by describing its exact location in the computer (drive and directory) and name (file name and extension).

FIXED DISK

Also referred to as a hard disk. A permanent disk inside the computer with a large capacity, usually greater than 10 megabytes.

MEMORY

The computer stores data and programs in electronic memory called RAM (temporary), or on disk (permanent). Memory is measured in bytes (a byte is a single character). A kilobyte (K) is 1,000 bytes and a megabyte (MB) is 1,000,000 bytes.

MICROPROCESSOR

An integrated circuit that is the brain of the computer. It contains the circuits required to perform calculations, process information and communicate with other parts of the computer such as the keyboard, disk drives, monitor and memory.

MODEM

A device that transmits computer data through the telephone line.

MULTILEVEL FILING SYSTEM

Permits a filing structure to be created containing many levels. Each level can contain multiple directories with paths to other levels or subdirectories. Each subdirectory can contain data and application program files. A multilevel filing system is also known as a hierarchical or tree structured filing system.

OPERATING SYSTEM

A computer program that controls and coordinates the computer hardware (CPU, disk drives, monitor, mouse, keyboard, printer) and communicates with the application software (WordPerfect, Lotus 1-2-3, etc.).

PATH

The path identifies the drive and route to take through the directory structure to get to the file location.

PROMPT

A symbol (typically C> or C:\>) displayed by the operating system to identify that the system is ready to accept a command.

RAM

RAM stands for Random Access Memory. DOS uses this memory to temporarily store working data and program information. The contents of RAM are lost when the power to the computer is removed or interrupted.

ROM

ROM stands for Read Only Memory. The computer uses this memory for routine tasks, such as starting up the machine. ROM contents are stored permanently, cannot be changed and are not lost when power to the computer is removed or interrupted.

ROOT DIRECTORY

The top or main directory created by DOS in a multi-level filing system.

SOFTWARE

Provides instructions and information in electronic form to direct the computer hardware.

SYSTEM PROMPT

When DOS is ready to accept a command it displays the letter of the current drive followed by a greater than sign (example C> or C:\>), unless otherwise specified.

TEXT

Characters such as uppercase and lowercase letters of the alphabet, numbers 0 through 9, and punctuation marks.

TEXT FILE

A file that contains readable text.

VOLUME LABEL

A name consisting of up to 11 characters that a user assigns to a disk for quick identification of its contents.

WILDCARD CHARACTER

A character that can take the place of any other character in a file name or extension. DOS has two of these characters—the question mark (?), which can represent any single character; and the asterisk (*), which can represent from one to all characters.

WRITE PROTECT

To prevent the information on a diskette from being deleted, changed or edited, the opening or small notch on the diskette is covered (for 5.25 inch diskettes) or opened (for 3.5 inch diskettes).

INDEX